Bringing the Montessori Approach to your Early Years Practice

This easy-to-read series provides an introduction to some of the most important early years philosophies and shows how they can be incorporated into your setting. Each book provides:

- An outline of the background to the approach

- Clear explanations of the relevance to contemporary thinking

- Suggestions to help you to plan a successful learning environment

- Examples of what the individual approach can look like in practice.

These convenient guides are essential to early years practitioners, students and parents who wish to fully understand what each approach means to their setting and children.

Have you ever wondered what the Montessori approach is all about and how it can be used to benefit the young children in your setting?

In this book Barbara Isaacs explains how the Montessori approach works and provides examples from schools and nurseries implementing Montessori principles. It includes guidance on planning and assessment methods and practical activities for practitioners to try.

This new edition has been fully updated to include:

- The role of the Montessori practitioner

D0317545

- An explanation of Montessori classroom management

- Links to the key commitments of the Early Years Foundation Stage (EYFS) and what they mean in Montessori settings

- Examples to show how the six areas of learning and development in the EYFS are supported by Montessori learning materials.

This convenient guide will help early years practitioners, students and parents to really understand what the Montessori approach means to their setting and children.

Barbara Isaacs is Academic Director at Montessori Centre International.

E

Montessori Approach

This second edition published 2010
by Routledge
2 Park Square, Milton Park, Abingdon, Oxon, OX14 4RN

Simultaneously published in the USA and Canada
by Routledge
711 Third Avenue, New York, NY 10017

Routledge is an imprint of the Taylor & Francis Group, an informa business

© 2010 Barbara Isaacs

Typeset in Optima by
Pindar NZ, Auckland, New Zealand
Printed and bound in Great Britain by
TJ International Ltd, Padstow, Cornwall

British Library Cataloguing in Publication Data
A catalogue record for this book is available from the British Library

Library of Congress Cataloging in Publication Data
Isaacs, Barbara, 1949-
  Bringing the montessori approach to your early years practice / by
Barbara Isaacs. — 2nd ed.
    p. cm.
  Includes bibliographical references.
  LB1029.M75I83 2010
  371.39'2—dc22   2009050225

ISBN10: 0-415-56425-5 (hbk)
ISBN10: 0-415-56424-7 (pbk)
ISBN10: 0-203-85079-3 (ebk)

ISBN13: 978-0-415-56425-0 (hbk)
ISBN13: 978-0-415-56424-3 (pbk)
ISBN13: 978-0-203-85079-4 (ebk)

Contents

Acknowledgements

Barbara Isaacs would like to thank the children and staff at Gorton Mount Primary school for giving her the opportunity to continue learning from them and to experience some of the conditions that must have inspired Montessori in her work. Special thanks go also to her Montessori colleagues at Montessori Centre International, particularly Sandra Morris-Coole and Berhane Dory, whose support as 'critical guides' continues to challenge her work; and to Tony, Adelle and Daniel, for their patience and indulgence of all my interests.

Thanks go also to children and staff from Iverna Gardens Montessori Nursery, Happy Days Montessori Nursery, Rosehouse Montessori Nursery and Seedlings Montessori Nursery for contributing photographs to this book and to Nadia Nasser, who photographed many of these images.

Introduction

In January 2007, we celebrated the centenary of the opening of the first Montessori nursery in Rome. I hope this book will extend awareness of the unique nature of this event and will help to explain the reasons why Montessori education remains so relevant to the lives of today's children, their parents and carers, and also the communities in which they live.

There is no doubt that Maria Montessori's pedagogy has made an impact on today's understanding of early years education and has influenced present-day good practice. That this contribution is not always recognised or attributed to Montessori may lie in the fact that, over the years and through the rapid expansion of early years services, we have often forgotten to reflect on and appreciate the roots from which the early years community has grown. The work of Friedrich Wilhelm Froebel, Rudolf Steiner, the Macmillan sisters and Susan Isaacs forms the foundation of our understanding of nursery education in today's Britain and highlights the need for an informed pedagogy that continues to evolve. Montessori herself refers in her writing to the work of Jean-Jacques Rousseau and Friedrich Wilhelm Froebel, as well as to two French educationalists, Edouard Seguin and Jean-Marc-Gaspard Itard. From her earliest writing, Montessori also makes links with developmental theorists of the day, such as Sigmund Freud and Jean Piaget. Tina Bruce makes a clear case for this considered approach:

> Until we are clear about the lenses through which we view children, we cannot begin to work effectively with them, nor is it easy to work in partnership with other practitioners or multi-agency colleagues,

parents or carers, because our assumptions about the child are crucial in influencing our practice.

(Bruce 2005: 2)

The Montessori approach is possibly best known today for the contribution it makes to our understanding of the importance of learning through the senses and the development of learning materials that are today referred to as 'educational toys', a new concept in Montessori's time. However, we need to understand that the materials, or apparatus as they were called by Montessori, are tools for children to reveal their 'true nature'. I believe that the key to the continued success of the Montessori approach lies in the unique relationship between the respect and trust in the child's ability to construct themselves within a 'favourable environment'. According to Montessori, this favourable environment offers children the opportunity to learn by following the unique rhythm of each child and being supported by sensitive, well-prepared adults, who respect the child's individuality. However, Montessori also highlights the important contribution all children make to our future and sees children as agents for potential social change through her vision of 'education for peace'. This vision is an essential part of her evolutionary approach to the education of children, which she called 'cosmic education'.

I hope this book will help to unravel some of the complex terminology Montessori uses and will make her writing more accessible to today's readers. It is important to see Montessori's writing from a historical perspective: most of her books consist of a series of lectures, speeches and presentations that were edited into books more than fifty years ago, and were translated from Italian. Her use of language seems somewhat archaic now and changes in our understanding and use of certain terms has contributed to uncertainty and controversy over her exact meaning as, for example, when she refers to 'deviations' or 'the normalisation of the child'. In addition, some of the terminology used in the last century is provocative to the readers of today, such as Montessori's reference (1964) to 'working with idiot children'. Nonetheless, the spirit of the child and her commitment to following the child remain constant throughout Montessori's writing, as does her reverence for children and her understanding that children hold our future in their hands.

I also hope this second edition will provide further insight into Montessori practice, particularly in relation to the Early Years Foundation Stage (EYFS) and its impact on early years practice in England today. From my perspective, the principles which underpin the EYFS follow in the footsteps of Maria Montessori by advocating support for the child as a unique individual, in enabling environments and within positive relationships. These are certainly conditions, which Montessori envisaged for children's development and learning.

The aim of this book is to explain the principle of *'following the child'* in the context of Montessori practice in the United Kingdom today and to explore the relevance of Montessori practice to the Early Years Foundation Stage.

1 | Background

This chapter looks briefly at Montessori's life and work; at her early start as a medical doctor; her first nursery, which she called 'Casa dei Bambini'; and her training of adults as Montessori teachers. All these elements of her career contributed to the rise of the Montessori International movement, which continues to thrive in the twenty-first century.

Maria Montessori's early life and study

Maria Montessori's own life is closely linked with the political, social and economic changes that resulted from the unification of Italy in the year Montessori was born, 1870. The political change also heralded social and economic change, but the process was slow as was inevitable in a country with a male-dominated electoral minority, large levels of illiteracy, and driven by the Catholic Church. The economic and social status of the population contributed to the continued struggle within Italian society. The division between the small group of wealthy and educated people and the large peasant population continued to undermine the political movement and ultimately led to the emergence of the fascist state led by Benito Mussolini. So this was the Italy into which Maria Montessori was born in Chiaravalle in the province of Ancona on 31 August 1870.

Maria was the only daughter of Alessandro Montessori and Renilde Stoppani. Alessandro's nationalistic and somewhat conservative outlook on life contrasted with the progressive and liberal Renilde, who was unusually well-educated for a girl born within the region. As a civil servant, Alessandro and his family were expected to move home many times. They finally settled in Rome in 1875 when Maria was five years old. This gave the family the opportunity to join the city's growing middle-classes where they had access to the culture and intellectual energy of this growing capital.

Maria joined the public school in Via de San Nicola da Tolentino at the age of six in 1876, the year before primary education had become compulsory in Italy. Anecdotes from devoted friends paint a picture of a determined and diligent young girl, untypical of her social class. Montessori preferred to follow the technical rather than the classical stream of education, reflected in her interest and love of mathematics and the opportunity taken to follow the 'modern curriculum' (Kramer 1976: 32).

By the time Montessori graduated at the age of twenty, she was interested in biological sciences and was determined to study medicine, a path not followed by a woman in Italy before. Having achieved the Diploma de License in the spring of 1892 with the high grade of 8 out of 10, Montessori was eligible to study medicine at the University of Rome. In her day, it was unthinkable for a woman to join the medical faculty where all the facilities were designed for men. It is not clear what intervention Montessori used to achieve her goal, but the fact is that in 1892, she did join the University as a medical student.

Montessori's years of study were challenging in every aspect: her father disapproved, she was ridiculed by her fellow students and she also hated dissection, which she had to perform in the evenings. In 1894, she won the Roti prize and the scholarship that accompanied it. By 1896, she started working both with children and women as well as attending the Regia psychiatric clinic. In the last year of her studies, like the rest of her fellow students, she gave a lecture to the class. She expected to be ridiculed. Instead her talk was well attended and received, and there was an extra bonus; it was attended by her father. Montessori's success had ended six years of rejection and criticism. She was much admired and celebrated. Montessori herself wrote to a friend in 1896: 'So here I am: famous! ... I am not famous because of my skill or intelligence, but for my courage and indifference. ... This is something which, if one wishes, one can always achieve, but it takes tremendous effort.'

In the same year, Montessori started her first appointment as the surgical assistant at San Spirito's hospital. She also helped in children's and women's hospitals and established her own private practice. Like many nineteenth-century women of her class, she felt social responsibility for the poor and supported them far beyond the duty expected from a physician. In 1897, she was asked to visit Rome's asylums, and this led to meeting the 'idiot children', who were to change her life. Montessori's experience of these children, collecting crumbs from the floor once they had eaten, had led her to consider the fact that perhaps they behaved in this way because they were bored. They had nothing to play with!

Montessori continued to be preoccupied with the fate of these children in the asylum and her encounter with the work of Jean-Marc-Gaspard Itard (born 1775) and his pupil Edouard Seguin (born 1812) gave some answers. Itard was and is best known for his study of the Wild Boy of Aveyron, a feral child, who was discovered running wild in the Aveyron wood. He decided to 'civilise the young man', to develop his senses and to gradually teach him to speak. Itard developed his own method for promoting the boy's language skills based on sensorial experiences and matching, pairing and sorting activities. Many of these teaching tools were to be used and developed by Montessori a hundred years later when she came to work with children in the first Casa dei Bambini in the San Lorenzo district of Rome.

Montessori also found inspiration in Edouard Seguin's work, which led her to believe 'that mental deficiency presented chiefly a pedagogical rather than medical problem' (Kramer 1976: 96). In the spring of 1900, the National League for Retarded Children opened the medical-pedagogical institute, a school for what today we call children with special needs. Montessori became the director with twenty-two children attending.

One of Montessori's co-directors of the institute, Dr Montessano, gradually became a close friend and lover. The result of this union was a son, Mario. Kramer (1976: 92) says: 'Everything we know about her makes it unbelievable that it could have been a casual liaison.' Mario was given his mother's name and went to a wet nurse after birth. It is hard to imagine the psychological impact this event had on Dr Montessori. At the beginning of the twentieth century, having a child out of wedlock would have been professional as well as social suicide. 'Deprived of the experience of caring for her own child, she was to turn her attention increasingly to meeting the needs of other children' (Kramer 1976: 93).

In 1900, Montessori again enrolled to study at the University of Rome. She continued her interest in psychology and pursued Seguin's theory of educating the senses through concrete experiences. In Naples in 1902, she presented her own ideas about the possibility of the education of 'unteachable children'. She made links between the two theories, exploring the notion of training of the senses and the importance of approaching abstraction through concrete forms a child could see and touch (Kramer 1976). This was the basis for later development of the Montessori apparatus and sensorial materials that she called 'materialised abstractions'.

One of her students of the time and a later friend and collaborator was Anna Maccheroni, who recalled (in Kramer 1976: 97–98) Montessori's lectures: 'She was a most attractive lecturer; her language was so simple, so clear, her delivery so animated, that even the poorer students could understand her. All that she said had the warmth of life.'

The first Montessori nursery

In 1906, Montessori was asked to look after children of migrant workers, who lived in the tenements of the San Lorenzo district of Rome. The rationale for the project was simple: while the parents worked and older children attended school, the three to six-year-olds roamed the streets and got up to mischief. The developers, who owned the tenements, decided to contain these children in a room and invited Dr Montessori to take charge of them. As the funding for this project was non-existent, Montessori furnished the room with small tables and chairs rather than desks, a selection of modified materials originally used with her 'idiot children', and she employed the porter's daughter to look after these fifty or so street urchins. Two of the revolutionary classrooms were set up and Montessori herself was actively involved for two years. Her work with these children laid a foundation for what we know today as the Montessori approach to education.

The first Casa dei Bambini opened in 58 Via dei Marsai, San Lorenzo,

Rome on 6 January 1907. From the beginning, Montessori observed the children's reactions to their new environment without any pre-conceived ideas of what would happen. These observations provided opportunities to understand better the children and the materials themselves – this was, what we call today, action research. She modified the materials in relation to the children's use, adapting them further for the use of children without learning difficulties. Montessori's observations gave her a further insight into the nature of children and formed the basis of the discoveries explained in her first book *The Montessori Method*, which was published in Rome in 1912. In this book, Montessori described children as:

- being capable of extended periods of concentration;

- enjoying repetition and order;

- revelling in the freedom of movement and choice;

- enjoying purposeful activities (preferred work to play);

- self-motivated, displaying behaviours that did not require either punishments or rewards;

- taking delight in silence and harmony of the environment;

- possessing personal dignity and spontaneous self-discipline;

- being capable of learning to read and write.

It was these discoveries that made Montessori believe that these characteristics represented the potential of humanity. She advocated that all children should be given the opportunity to 'reveal themselves' in a developmentally appropriate environment that would facilitate their natural growth and development.

Both E. M. Standing (1984) and Rita Kramer (1976) document the history of the rise of the Montessori approach in great detail in their books. Both authors give a unique insight into this social and pedagogical experiment that Montessori herself described as follows on the occasion of the opening of the second Children's House:

This is not simply a place where the children are kept, ... but a true school for their education. … We have put the school within the home … We have placed it within the home as the property of the community … The idea of the community ownership of the school is new and very beautiful and profoundly educational. The parents know that the Casa dei Bambini is their property and is maintained by a portion of the rent they pay. Mothers can go at any hour of the day to watch …

(Montessori in Kramer 1976: 123)

For Montessori, the Casa dei Bambini was a tool for social change for both children and their mothers, and in this inaugural speech, she also related to maternal functions and the need and opportunities for women to work and have their children in care of 'the directress [Montessori's name for the teacher] and the house physician' (Kramer 1976: 124). Here, Kramer expresses her view that Montessori may possibly reflect on her own 'inability to mother her child' and her concern for the quality of care to be given to children of absent mothers. This dilemma continues to haunt today's working mothers.

There is no doubt that the children thrived and parents appreciated their children's growing awareness of hygiene, good manners, as well as independence and opportunities to learn. The reputation of this pedagogical experiment spread rapidly, thanks to the growing affordability of newsprint. Within the next two years, the Children's Houses had many Italian and foreign visitors with dignitaries and teachers coming from all over the world.

International Montessori movement

Montessori decided in 1913 to give up both her lectureship at the university and in the medical profession. From then on, she would devote her energies to the training of Montessori teachers, to the development of Montessori learning materials and to the establishment of the Montessori network worldwide. Between 1907 and 1914, when World War 1 broke out, interest in Montessori education flourished and many opportunities were opened to Montessori to promote her unique view of children and their learning. By 1914, there were hundreds of Montessori schools established in Europe, North and South America as well as India, Sri Lanka and Pakistan.

For the next forty years, Montessori continued to travel, lecture and promote Montessori education. She visited all the continents and left us a legacy from which thousands and thousands of children around the globe benefited. She died in the Netherlands at the end of the summer of 1952, wanting to be known as a citizen of the world.

2 | The Montessori approach

This chapter explores what is generally understood by the Montessori approach today. Montessori describes children's development in stages, each one unique and essential in the maturation of the child. Each stage should be supported by an environment, which supports the unique qualities of the child and which also includes adults and peers, who contribute significantly to the environment and therefore to the children's learning. The Montessori approach to education has three key components:

1. the child;
2. the favourable environment;
3. the teacher.

The relationship between the child, teacher and environment continues to evolve and develop because it is based on observation of children. The evolving links between all three components and their interaction represent what we know today as the Montessori approach.

The child

Montessori recognises and celebrates the unique individuality of each child and the potential that they hold within themselves. She urges adults to demonstrate trust in the child's ability to learn and absorb the

environment and the culture in which they grow up, and so become an adult. She sees the child as the possible agent in affecting social change on this planet.

Montessori believed that children develop in stages or planes and that each stage has its own unique qualities and characteristics. The child's needs have to be reflected in the environment and in the strategies employed by the adults when facilitating their learning.

Each stage is heralded by physical changes in the body, particularly of the teeth: loss of milk teeth around six, loss of molars at around twelve and emergence of wisdom teeth around the age of eighteen, when adulthood begins. The three stages are:

1. the absorbent mind – conception to six (birth to three: unconscious absorbent mind; three to six: conscious absorbent mind);

2. childhood – six to twelve (considered to be calm and conducive to learning);

3. adolescence – twelve to eighteen (twelve to fifteen is as unpredictable as the first stage).

The age bands are approximate and provide very flexible developmental guidelines, while recognising the uniqueness of each child.

The absorbent mind

The absorbent mind is a time of enormous potential in the development of the individual. Human beings need stimulation and opportunity to develop the brain through active learning and exploration, and refinement through our senses. The fundamental principle of this stage is recognition of the child as a spontaneous learner, driven by an inner drive/energy that Montessori (1988a) termed 'horme'. The Greek word refers to the child's drive from within to learn from the environment – what Bruce (2005) refers to as self-motivation.

Characteristic of the absorbent mind are three embryonic stages or, as Montessori (1988a) puts it, 'periods of rebirth':

- physical embryo – when the child's physical body is formed in the womb, the pre-natal stage of life;

- spiritual embryo – the period after birth, when the unique nature of the human being, individual to each child, emerges. Montessori often talks of the child's emerging personality in relation to this embryonic stage;

- social embryo – when the child is ready to embrace the social aspects of their life, gradually becoming aware of the social conventions of their culture and of the needs and feelings of others.

During the first stage of life, we witness children acquiring certain skills and abilities. Montessori terms these predispositions 'sensitive periods'. They emerge from the 'human tendencies' (Montessori 1988a), the inherited traits, characteristic of all human beings, such as orientation, communication, gregariousness, creativity and imagination. The 'sensitive periods' (Montessori 1966) unfold when, and if, the conditions of the child's environment are favourable.

There are six key sensitive periods:

1. order

2. movement

3. small details

4. language

5. refinement of the senses

6. the social aspects of life.

It is the manifestations of the sensitive periods on which the prime carer or teacher should focus as they observe, so that they can provide appropriate learning opportunities for the child. Montessori believed that if appropriate support from the adult is not available, opportunities will be lost or the child will miss out on developing to their full potential. Sensitive periods are universal, evident in all children around the world. They are also present within the child at birth and can be concurrent and 'run parallel to each other'. Each sensitive period reaches its peak at a different time during the first six years of life. For example, the sensitive period for language starts in the womb when the baby recognises their mother's voice. Babies are pre-disposed to respond to human language. They listen attentively before their first word is uttered. Then between eighteen and thirty-six months, the child's language explodes, from passive to active vocabulary, ability to use grammar and syntax, using language appropriately within the social context and manipulating it to demonstrate a sense of humour. However, if children are not exposed to opportunities to hear rich language used in the context of everyday life, the potential of their ability to communicate effectively will be limited by the lack of experience.

The sensitive period for order is evident from birth and reflects the baby's need for routines that provide predictability and consistency from which a sense of security emerges. As the child grows, they will be able to orientate themselves within the home through familiar arrangements and the child will adapt to them. For example, when going for a walk, we may be surprised by the toddler's ability to 'find the way' to the public library. It is their sensitive period for order that helps them to absorb the route we have taken on many previous occasions when visiting the library. By the time they are two/two-and-a-half, they will be able to find toys in their room and be also able to replace them where found. The external order will be supporting their initiative as well as organisational skills and problem solving. These are just two of the above-mentioned sensitive periods. You can read more about the children's sensitive periods in *The Secret of Childhood* and *The Absorbent Mind* (Montessori 1966 and 1988a), Lillard's *Montessori, the Modern Approach* (1972) and Standing's *Montessori, Her Life and Work* (1984).

Montessori (1988a) defines the absorbent mind as operating at two levels:

1. the 'unconscious level' in the first three years of life, when the children are absorbing indiscriminately from the environment that surrounds them; at the time when sensitive periods for order, movement, small detail and language feature prominently in the child's development;

2. the 'conscious level' reflecting the child's growing ability to organise and classify information, experiences and concepts. This stage of the absorbent mind is closely linked with the child's sensitive period for refinement of the senses and social aspects of life. It is supported by the sensitive periods for order and small details.

Childhood

This is the second stage of the child's development, which Montessori (1994) defined as the calm stage, when the child is very keen to learn and eager to belong to a group. The characteristic sensitive periods exhibited during this plane relate to the child's moral development and acquisition of culture. (Note that from Montessori's point of view, culture includes not only a set of social conventions and experiences. It also relates to areas of learning such as natural sciences, history and geography).

Adolescence

This third plane of development is seen by Montessori as comparable with the first stage of life, with its turbulence and unpredictability and volatility. It is further subdivided into puberty (twelve to fifteen years of age) when Montessori acknowledges the big physical changes that take place within the child's body, and likens it to the time of the spiritual embryo when adults need to exercise a great deal of patience and understanding in support of children of this age. The second sub-stage of this period is termed adolescence (from fifteen to eighteen). Here Montessori highlights the young person's need to find a group of friends with whom they can identify.

Montessori's views on education during childhood and adolescence can be found in *From Childhood to Adolescence* (1994). Montessori teachers in the United States and Sweden have developed her ideas on education of teenagers further and David Khan has written extensively on this topic for the North American Montessori Association, whilst Lillard (1996) explores the education of primary age children in *Montessori Today*.

Montessori also refers to a fourth stage of development that relates to the early stages of adulthood (eighteen to twenty-four years of age). However, she does not discuss any new or significant insights into the lives of young adults. In this book, I will focus on children between birth and the age of six in the absorbent mind plane of development, with particular emphasis on the second stage of this plane, the three to six-year-olds.

The favourable environment

Rationale for the favourable environment

Montessori, just like Piaget (1962), saw the environment as a key factor in children's spontaneous learning. She believed it should be favourable to the development of the whole child, and should offer opportunities for the development of the potential of each individual. When Montessori described the favourable environment, she saw the child as an active agent of this environment, and the teacher as the facilitator of the child's learning and development. It is the role of the teacher to ensure that the environment provides for the developmental needs of each individual child. Observation serves as the key tool for identification of these developmental needs.

As the child responds to the stimuli within a given environment, be it home, school or nursery, the adults present should observe and interpret behaviour according to the sensitive periods and maturation of the child. With this in mind, they should ensure that the activities, materials, objects and occupations in the environment are brought to the attention of the child to facilitate, scaffold and extend learning opportunities for the child. Adults, as well as the child's peers, act to some extent as a catalyst in the maturation process, while the materials, objects and occupations within the environment scaffold the child's learning (see the work of Bruner (1960) and Vygotsky (1978) for more detail about scaffolding).

Qualities of the favourable environment

Now that we have looked at Montessori's view of the characteristics of children in different age groups, we can examine the Montessori favourable environment. This environment must be, above all, safe for the child. Here, the nursery will follow given government guidelines, and in the English context, the Early Years Foundation Stage (DCFS 2008) document provides 'the statutory framework' for safeguarding of children.

From the Montessori perspective, the favourable environment is characterised by:

- accessibility and availability;
- freedom of movement and choice;
- personal responsibility;
- reality and nature;
- beauty and harmony.

Accessibility and availability

The first Children's House was designed as the house of children, therefore everything in the room was prepared with children in mind. Some aspects of the environment such as the lack of desks and a teacher's table, and the child-friendly size of the furniture, which were revolutionary in Montessori's day, have become accepted practice of all good early years provision. It is also recognised that many children of this age benefit from open floor space that can be used for a variety of individual or group activities, as many young children do not particularly enjoy sitting at a table. Montessori also advocated that the garden or outdoor space has a covered terrace that would give children opportunities to be inside or outside in any weather conditions – this was her contribution to the currently popular model for the outdoor classroom.

The organisation of the materials, activities and occupations on open shelving, according to areas of learning and representing the areas of learning as defined by the Montessori early years curriculum (further explained in Chapter 3), is another aspect of the favourable environment that offers availability and accessibility. These materials are usually arranged in a specific order, setting out a possible sequence that the child may or may not choose to adopt. This sequence follows the growing complexity of the activities and the gradual building of specific skills and so scaffolds the child's learning. Each activity is presented on a tray, in a basket or in a box, with all the resources complete and available in a self-contained manner. Once a child selects it from the shelf, they should have all the resources necessary for that activity. This completeness provides for focused work and lack of distraction once the occupation has been chosen. Generally, each activity has its place in the classroom in order to support the child's freedom of choice and the sensitive period for order. This facilitates consistency and predictability within the environment. It is the teacher's role to ensure the consistency and predictability of the environment are maintained.

Freedom of movement and choice

The favourable environment that provides children with a wide range of accessible and available activities, designed to meet their individual needs, will also support the child's need for freedom. To facilitate freedom, teachers need to have trust and respect the child. Only if this trust and respect are embedded in the daily routines can the children have true freedom of movement and choice; these two freedoms are inseparable. Children can only make appropriate choices if they have the opportunity to move around the room and find what they need to satisfy their inner drive, or 'horme' (Montessori 1988a).

The environment needs to be predictable to facilitate the plans and choices made by the child. When children decide to do what they need to do, they are also able to take as much or as little time to do the activity as they choose. Many children will choose to repeat the same task over and over again, either on the same day or on subsequent days. This need for repetition often relates to the child's sensitive periods and is integral to the freedoms offered within Montessori classrooms, as is freedom from interruption. It is considered inappropriate to disturb a child deep in concentration on a specific self-chosen activity and according to Montessori (1988a and 1988b), it is the duty of the teacher to protect this child from interruption.

We must not forget that the child, who is 'free to do' also needs to be 'free not to do'. There are those children, who prefer to learn by watching others. Giving a child the time to sit and watch, or to contemplate a ray of sunlight, reflects our respect for the individual as much as the freedom to repeat an activity or the freedom to engage in an activity or play without interruption does.

Children also have freedom of speech, which relates directly to the sensitive period for language. The child's ability to express and communicate thoughts and ideas is considered to be an essential part of all pre-school provision, bearing in mind the stages of language development. The calm, purposeful atmosphere in a Montessori classroom contributes greatly towards children's developing communication skills.

Personal responsibility

However, all the freedoms of the nursery do not mean limitless licence for the child to do as they please. It is generally considered that freedom carries personal responsibility and therefore, there are some expectations the adults and peers have of the children, who access the freedoms of the favourable environment. The collective interest of the group must be considered first, so that children will be actively discouraged from any dangerous or hurtful acts that may endanger them or others.

The teachers and other children model appropriate and polite behaviour, both in communications and when using the activities available in the classroom. Children are expected to return their chosen activities back to the place where they are kept, complete and ready for another person to use; in other words, how they found them. This ability to return materials to the shelf may take quite a lot of modelling and consistency of expectation. A patient and creative approach from the adults, alongside the positive example set by older children, will be beneficial to the younger children, who may initially find it difficult to remember what is expected of them.

It is these responsibilities that also guide the child towards social awareness, the ability to share and what Montessori (1988a) calls the 'cohesion of the social unit'. Children mature into their social awareness, not only through the modelling of adults, but also from examples given by the other children in the group. The favourable environment supports children's individual progress, but it does not mean that the social aspects of life are unimportant. For Montessori, the Children's House offers family groupings of children, allowing the older, more settled children to model behaviour. They also have the opportunity to become 'teachers' when a younger child needs help or wants to know how to use an activity. The older children are often the first ones to remind the younger ones to put away their activity, or to help them with tasks such as putting on shoes or a coat.

In the Montessori classroom, we witness many displays of attentive empathy as well as giving the younger children time to try things on their own. This peer support spontaneously emerges and is seldom prompted by the adults in the classroom. From the point of view of the younger child, it seems so much more sensible to be able to follow the lead of a peer whom you admire rather than be guided by the adult. It is quite common for the older children to share activities with the younger ones and to help them where appropriate. From this spontaneous support for one another grows a unity of the group, which heightens awareness of courteous behaviour, kindness and generosity among the group. 'This unity born among the child, which is produced by a spontaneous need directed by an unconscious power, and vitalized by a social spirit, is a phenomenon needing a name, and I call it "cohesion of the social unit"' (Montessori 1988a: 212).

Reality and nature

It is imperative that the materials and activities available on the shelves reflect the children's growing developmental needs as well as their interests, and are real or three-dimensional models rather than two-dimensional pictorial representations. For example, if we speak about shells, plants, skeletons or stethoscopes, it is best to have these objects actually present in the classroom to encourage their exploration through the senses and the extension of vocabulary. This approach is also advocated by the recently published *First Hand Experience, What Matters to Children* (Rich *et al.* 2005) and as part of the rich learning opportunities offered by the 'Forest Schools Programme' (started in Denmark in 1950s).

To cite another example, the Montessori sensorial materials include a selection of solid (such as a cube, cone and pyramid) and flat shapes (such as a triangle, square and circle), all made of wood, which the child can explore and use to absorb the properties of these shapes. These materials serve as a springboard for exploration of everyday objects with these properties, both found in the classroom as well as at home and in the wider environment.

As it is the teacher who is the custodian of the environment, they ensure that the classroom reflects nature by finding ways of including fresh flowers in the classroom, by offering opportunities for observation of nature both inside and outside the classroom, and by ensuring that the nature table reflects not only the seasons, but also the interests of the children; that it is vibrant and alive and enticing. The nature table

23

(sometimes referred to as the project table) should also offer opportunities for children to contribute towards the daily life of the classroom. Children should be given regular opportunities to explore nature through gardening and nature walks, and the 'outdoor classroom' should offer these activities as part of the learning programme.

Beauty and harmony

Another important feature of the favourable environment is its beauty and harmony. Montessori (1988b) felt very strongly that the environment has to be pleasing, so as to invite the child to activity. She also felt that the materials, activities and occupations should entice the child and for this reason, all other decorations within the room are kept very simple, so as not to distract the child's attention. This simplicity also means that the child is able to act autonomously within the environment, not only choosing activities, but also having the ability to wash up after snack time, clean the easel after painting, wipe the table should anything get spilled and so on. The child's ability to contribute towards the care of the environment is seen as one of the contributing factors to freedom with responsibility.

The harmony of the environment is represented by the organisation of the classroom and also by the purposeful, quiet atmosphere in which children are engaged in self-chosen activities corresponding to their needs. This is one of the fundamental differences between a Montessori classroom and other early years provision – the calmness of the classroom is often commented upon by visitors and teachers are asked how it is achieved. It is the self-directed nature of the activities that promotes this harmony; if the children are truly free to choose what they need to do and are not coerced into doing things simply because adults ask them to, it is more likely that they will be engaged, able to concentrate and ultimately satisfied with the outcomes of the activities. Generally, the Montessori classroom is a hum of activity; not silent, but not loud and chaotic, characterised by children engaged in activities working on their own, with a friend or in small groups, depending on their age, interest and abilities.

The beauty of the environment symbolises the teachers' commitment to the respect for the children in their care. The adults ensure that materials are kept in excellent condition and that their own behaviour is gracious and polite. In fact, the classroom for three to six-year-olds should truly be a Casa dei Bambini – Children's House – a place in which children are comfortable, relaxed and feel at home so that they can reveal their true nature (Montessori 1988a).

Outcomes of the favourable environment

Montessori observed children in the classroom working on their own and in small groups, some being quick and others taking time to repeat an activity several times, each following their own rhythm. Bearing in mind that within one classroom there may be three-, four- and five-year-olds, we also need to acknowledge that any timetable for the morning would be inappropriate because it would disturb the natural rhythm of the individual children. The span of the morning, usually a three-hour period, is what Montessori termed the *work cycle.*

During this time, children will engage in a variety of activities, and if this period is not interrupted by an arbitrary adult-imposed schedule, the child will have time to reveal their natural tendencies and sensitive periods. It is wonderful to observe children, who know the classroom well, entering in the morning. As soon as they have got themselves ready for the day and said goodbye to their parents and carers, they select an activity. For some, this first task is always the same; it may be painting, a puzzle, a book or a writing task. It may be that way for a week or two, perhaps a month and then it changes, reflecting the child's growing interests and developing sensitive periods. Usually this activity helps children to 'settle into the routine of the day'.

The child then proceeds to select other activities, each following the same pattern – making a conscious choice, taking the activity to a chosen place, working with it, putting it back into its container and replacing it on the shelf. This we call the *cycle of activity.* Within any morning, the child will conduct many cycles of activity and will do some of them on their own, others with friends and others with the adults in the environment. As the morning progresses, the child usually gets involved in one or two activities that will particularly engage their concentration, and then there will be times when the child begins to wander, finding it more difficult to make a choice.

Montessori (1991) believed it was important to give the child the time to find what they need. She warned adults against interrupting the child during 'the false fatigue' (the time of search for the next activity). The child needs to be able to select each activity by themselves in order to be able to engage in an activity that meets their individual needs, to help them become involved and engaged in what they are doing. Montessori (1988a) speaks of the child using their volition. These periods of concentrated work interspersed with times of searching are described by Montessori as the *curve of work*. Careful observations of each child should produce evidence of a particular curve of work unique to the individual. The more focused and settled the child is, the longer the periods of engagement are and the shorter the false fatigue is. Montessori warns teachers against stepping in and interrupting the false fatigue as this undermines the child's volition. The teacher who is afraid of losing control of the class (in other words, who does not trust the children) replaces the children's will with their own decision to do something with a group or suggests having a snack or going outside, so imposing their own timetable on the natural rhythm of the individual children. The curve of work is an ideal tool for recording of any free-flow of activity (Bruce 2003), currently promoted as optimum mode for learning.

The child, who benefits from the extended work cycle and the freedom within the limits of the favourable environment, will gradually be able to exercise a certain amount of self-control. First, by putting an activity away; then, by thinking of others as they clean the snack table ready for others to use; and finally, by having sufficient self-control to be able to share a game with a child, or be able to say 'You have it now, I am happy to wait.' This process of maturation takes time and could be compared to trekking in the mountains, up and down, with some days being easier than others. Gradually, over a period of time, the child develops self-discipline, having experienced the richness of the environment, compassion, generosity, trust and respect of the adults and peers, having had the time and the opportunities to know themselves. It is the child with these characteristics whom Montessori (1988a) calls the 'normalised child'. She used this term, with its admittedly problematic connotation in today's usage, to describe a child who follows the normal/natural path of development; a child who has developed physically; who has had the opportunity to develop their personality; and who has also experienced rich learning opportunities as well as the benefits of being part of a social group.

The teacher

The learning materials developed by Montessori represent the foundation of the favourable environment, prepared for children. However, it is the teacher's duty, based on their observations of individual children, to add, complement or develop these materials to meet the individual's needs. It is incredible that these materials, developed almost one hundred years ago, remain relevant and engaging for children today. However, they must not be seen as the only requirements of the classroom; just as Montessori modified and continuously developed the activities offered to the children of her day, so the Montessori teachers of today have a duty to extend the range of materials on offer. These additions should reflect and complement the principles on which the original materials were developed. This requires well-informed practitioners, who have a sound understanding of not only the materials, but also of child development, both from the Montessori perspective as well as from the point-of-view of current developmental theory.

It is also expected that Montessori teachers reflect upon their work with children and are able to share their thoughts and understanding of children with their colleagues and parents. It is my understanding that this reflective practice is an aspect of what Montessori (1988a and 1988b) herself called the spiritual preparation of the teacher. Further elements which, according to Montessori (1988b), contribute towards this preparation are humility, and respect for humanity and the planet. Wolf (1996) offers further insights into the spiritual nature of the Montessori approach including the preparation of the teacher.

All children have potential, curiosity and interest in engaging in social interaction, establishing relationships, constructing their learning, and

engaging with much of what the environment offers them. Teachers need to be deeply aware of the children's potential and ensure the environment responds to the children's needs and interests.

When considering the 'normalised' child, we must also consider the role of the teacher as a key factor in preparation and maintenance of this favourable environment and so indirectly helping the child follow their natural path of development. Throughout this chapter, I have already referred to aspects of the teacher's role in the preparation of the favourable environment and I will now reflect on the unique nature of the teacher as a facilitator of the child's learning.

Montessori (1988a and 1988b) described the teacher as the *director/directress*; as the one who, like the film director, oversees all that is happening in the classroom in order for the child to be able to learn spontaneously. While Montessori may have had this focus in mind, it is also evident that many Montessori teachers see their role today as facilitators; they guide and help children's access to the classroom resources. This is where the teacher makes the link between the environment and its materials and the child. This link is understood to be an active one in terms of the preparation and accessibility of the classroom, but a passive one in terms of the conventional teaching role.

Montessori saw the child and their spontaneous interest in the environment as the key to the learning process. Therefore, she speaks of the child's auto-education or the child's ability to teach themselves through the carefully prepared environment. This approach requires a change in the attitudes of the adults, who work with small children. First and foremost, it requires implicit trust in the child's ability to select activities relevant to their stage of development and also trust and understanding of the materials available to the child. The teacher must be confident in knowing that whatever is on offer in the classroom has a specific purpose that will benefit the child in some aspect of their development.

It also requires an adult, who will be able to help the children settle into the environment, to show them how it works and what it has to offer, and then to withdraw when the child is able to access the activities on their own. This approach gives children the opportunity to observe, explore and investigate the activities in the environment. This does not mean that the teacher abandons the child; they continue to observe and will lend a hand should the child need it, possibly suggesting a different approach or asking another child to offer help. The teacher may also join the child once an activity has been completed, so that they can talk about what the child discovered or why they approached the problem in a certain way, or admire the outcome. However, Montessori warns us about interruption of the child, who is concentrating on a task as this interruption may disturb a train of thought or the moment when a problem is just about to be solved. Montessori sees this interruption as undermining the child's efforts.

The teacher's role changes from an active one to that of a more passive facilitator. This is referred to by Standing (1984: 302–4), rather confusingly, as 'transference of activity'. The teacher continues to modify the environment for individual children through observation and occasional lessons. The lessons are offered when the child is ready to be introduced to new areas of the classroom or aspects of their learning.

Alongside consistent and skilful observation, this change of role is the biggest challenge for the Montessori teacher; at any one time, there are children in the classroom, who require more active interactions, while some will be less dependent and others will themselves become the teachers of the younger children. This is where the teacher's ability to observe, reflect upon and interpret children's behaviour will be their most useful tools. These observations will also serve as a means of record-keeping and assessment and to inform any planning and modification of the environment.

Many adults are attracted to Montessori teaching by her vision of the child as an autonomous learner and our own desire to share what we know with children. It is inevitable that these two aspects of our motivation will be in conflict with each other and how each teacher resolves this conflict results in the quality of Montessori provision.

The preparation of the teacher that Montessori talks about in her writings (1964, 1966, 1988a) requires sound knowledge of the Montessori philosophy as well as pedagogy, incorporating aspects of these two disciplines to developing observational skills and teaching strategies, as well as knowledge and understanding of how children develop and learn.

The Montessori teacher will also engage in supporting the families of the children attending the setting. A close partnership is required if the child is to benefit from the Montessori approach. Montessori herself recognised that both the nursery and the home have to share the values of *'following the child'* if we are to nurture the true potential of the whole child.

Inevitably the teachers of today, and of the future, will also need to know about the current legislation and requirements for caring for young children, as well as being familiar with the current trends in early years education and care. Like all teachers, the Montessori teacher will have to be committed to continued learning, as teaching is also a process of learning.

Montessori's vision of future Montessori teachers was that of well-trained individuals, committed to continuous learning. She also wanted teachers to be humble and open individuals, respecting the child as a unique human being.

3 | The Montessori early years curriculum

This chapter focuses on the Montessori early years curriculum and describes Montessori's views of children's learning as intrinsically linked with their development. It also identifies the key areas of learning found in Montessori early years settings. These areas of learning are defined by the activities and occupations identified and designed by Montessori (1965 and 1988b) as significant or essential in development of children's skills and capabilities.

Learning is holistic

For Montessori (1988a, 1988b), learning is a key to children's development and education as the main contributing factor to the child's preparation for life. However, she also recognises that young children do not learn subjects, but that their learning is integrated and holistic in its nature. The child's ability to observe, explore, investigate, ask questions, share ideas and so learn about the world is not necessarily organised into lessons or subjects. The child observes and explores when they become interested, when they are able to engage in an activity, which involves their whole being.

This child needs an adult, who is able to respond to their investigations wherever and whenever they occur – be it during bath-time, while listening to a story, on a walk, when digging in the garden or during a lesson. A responsive adult will try to answer, question, wonder or observe with the child and together they may discover some of the answers. The child may also need adults, who listen to their hypotheses, discoveries and investigations and simply smile or nod in response, or adults, who model skills and behaviours.

Therefore, if we wish to define the early years curriculum, we need to recognise that in the early years, 'learning occurs constantly whether intentionally or incidentally' (MacLeod-Brunell 2004: 45). We need to examine not only what the child learns but also how, in order to appreciate the complexities of learning in the early years.

Play is the best tool for learning

It is also generally agreed today that play is the most effective tool for the child's learning (Bruce 1991; Jenkinson 2002; Moyles 2005). Here, we have to try to unravel one of the big Montessori conundrums. Early on, in the first Children's House, Montessori discovered that children preferred work to play, and so throughout her writings, she refers to children working rather than playing.

This emphasis on work as opposed to play has constituted one of the key criticisms of the Montessori legacy by the early years community. It is

important to try to understand what Montessori herself meant. Her observations of children led her to the understanding that the nature of the child's work is fundamentally different to the nature of the adult's work. According to Montessori (1988a), the child is interested in the process whereas the adult is interested in the product. The child is happy to repeat the process; they are perfecting their skills through repetition. Just think of a three-year-old, who is helping to wash up, standing at the sink and washing the same plate over and over again. They wash it, put it on the draining board and then take it back off and wash it again. The result may not be perfect. However, the repetition serves as a tool of achieving competence and, in turn, of the construction of the human being.

'A child is also a worker and producer. Although he cannot share in the work of adults, he has his own difficult and important task to perform, that of producing a man' (Montessori 1966: 193). This quotation reflects another perspective on the work-versus-play debate. Montessori recognised the enormous task all children undertake within the developmental process of growing-up and maturing. She saw this to be the child's work. According to Montessori, all the activities within the classroom contribute to the child's development. So when children engage in these activities, they are working towards 'the creation/construction of man'.

This philosophical perspective on the nature of the child should be considered every time Montessori speaks in earnest of the child's work. I believe Montessori's emphasis on work needs to be seen as the child's need to do, to be active, to manipulate and so to learn – it does not negate the importance of play. For her, play is the child's work, but we must also acknowledge that children enjoy doing work and young children do not usually distinguish between work and play. Adults usually associate work with effort, and play with fun. However, we must also acknowledge the enormous effort evident in sustained play, which engages the whole child and culminates in feelings of satisfaction, joy and competence. This sense of well-being is usually associated with well-accomplished tasks related to work.

We also need to consider the historical perspective of Montessori's writing. Her discoveries, on which the majority of her writing is based, were made in the early twentieth century. At this time, there was little psychological knowledge about children. Montessori's ideas were formulated before Melanie Klein (1882–1960) and Anna Freud (1895–1982) developed their thoughts about play therapy; before A. S. Neil (1883–1973) set up the Summerhill school, or John Holt (1967) wrote *How Children Learn*. Montessori's own life bears testimony to the importance of diligence and hard work if we want to achieve anything as individuals. Therefore, it is not surprising that she focuses so much on work and the task of self-construction and means of self-fulfilment.

Furthermore, it is important to highlight that many of today's Montessori practitioners would acknowledge the importance of play in the lives of children. The present-day training of Montessori teachers explores the issues relating to the nature of the child's work and play. Children themselves relate to work in their play such as when pretending to be their parents or when they come to early years settings ready to do 'work'.

In the context of the Montessori classroom, it is up to the practitioners to understand the nature of the child's self-construction and not to differentiate between play and work, just as the child does not – they are simply keen to do things! Competent practitioners should be able to interpret the child's learning and development as documented in their observations. They should be able to explain the value and benefits of all the materials, activities and occupations available to the children in the classroom. These activities could be teacher-led or child-initiated. They could also evolve spontaneously or with sensitive support from the activities available on the shelves, demonstrating creativity and imagination.

Montessori areas of learning

Whether we call it work or play, the activities in the Montessori classroom have clearly defined aims and so contribute to the child's development and learning. For Montessorians, these activities represent the curriculum; a curriculum which is led by the interests of the individual, supported by peers and adults in the environment.

Montessori learning for babies and toddlers

In most Montessori environments for babies and toddlers, you will find children engaged in activities, which support development of physical skills and sensory experiences. Heuristic play is encouraged using treasure baskets and heuristic bags, in support of their spontaneous engagements. Songs, rhymes, stories and books are part of the daily routines, as are opportunities to be independent at mealtimes and basic hygiene. The children spend much time outside the classroom playing with water, sand, pushing trolleys, riding on bicycles and climbing slides. Simple puzzles and manipulative toys such as posting and sequencing boxes are available on open shelves. Toys, which encourage walking such as trolleys and prams, are available alongside walking platforms accessible from two or three steps. All these activities promote walking and balancing skills at an early age. Early practical life and sensorial activities and language activities, supporting development of vocabulary, are available to the older toddlers.

Practitioners should respect the children's natural rhythms as reflected in their individual routines. There should be opportunities for spontaneous nap time, quiet play, independent snack and outdoor play throughout the day.

Learning is planned on an individual basis with daily routines, such as nap time, rest time and meal time, contributing significantly to the child's learning about their world and about the relationships with adults and peers.

Currently, there are only a handful of Montessori environments for babies and toddlers, which adhere to Montessori practice for this age group described by Montanaro (1991) and Lillard and Lillard Jessen (2003) as infant communities.

Many Montessori day-care settings with provision for three months to five-year-olds adopt mainstream practice in their baby and toddler rooms, whilst focusing on Montessori provision for the two to five-year-olds. This trend has been reflected in the accreditation of Montessori nurseries as delivered by the Montessori Accreditation and Evaluation Board during 2008 and 2009.

Montessori learning for three to six-year-olds

During the past fifteen years, we have seen a significant change in Montessori early years environments. The Government's funding of pre-school provision for all three to four-years-olds has resulted in the majority of maintained schools offering reception class places to children in the September after their fourth birthday, mirroring the trend of the successful pre-preparatory schools. Combined with the compulsory school age, which in England is in the term after the child's fifth birthday, we find that most Montessori nurseries now offer places to two-year-olds and see these children leave at the age of four. However, the curriculum described below relates to the education of children from two and a half/ three to six years of age.

As mentioned in Chapter 2, in the description of the favourable environment for three to six-year-olds, the Montessori areas of learning broadly correspond with the physical organisation of the classroom for:

- practical life (or daily living);

- refinement of the senses;

- communication, language and literacy;

- numeracy and arithmetic;

- cultural aspects of life (or 'knowledge and understanding of the world' in the foundation stage curriculum);

- creativity.

Practical life

The activities in this area reflect the children's need to model behaviours reflecting their family life. They also allow children to contribute towards the cultural and social life of the classroom, offering them the opportunity to experience a sense of belonging.

One of the aims of the practical life activities is to make a link between the home and the new environment of the Montessori classroom. This

is done by representing tasks and activities with which children may be already familiar from their home environment such as pouring, dusting, getting dressed, sweeping the classroom or leaves in the garden and so on.

While they are carrying out these activities, the children perfect basic skills that will aid their independence both in the classroom as well as at home. They learn to pour their own drinks, serve food, tidy their own activities, wash their hands, wash up after their snack, water and tend to the plants inside and outside the classroom, feed the pets and many more skills. The main aim of any practical life activity is to develop and perfect skills that will contribute towards the child's autonomy.

Another aim common to all practical life activities is their active nature. Children manipulate and so perfect their gross and fine motor skills as well as coordination of movement, hand–eye coordination, dexterity and pincer grip. Just imagine the range of physical skills required to use pegs, scissors, tongs or tweezers, to plant a seed, to rake the lawn or to offer a snack to a friend. These skills contribute further to their autonomy.

They enhance the child's sense of belonging by providing them with skills, which contribute to the daily routines and upkeep of the classroom – such as washing their plate and glass after a snack or sweeping leaves in the garden.

The orderly nature of these activities supports the child's need to exert control over their environment and enhance their sense of well-being by the predictable and consistent nature of their organisation.

All the activities in this area of learning enhance children's ability to concentrate, to organise, sequence and order the activity, and to pay attention to detail, such as replacing utensils at the end of an activity.

Consider the following example of a two-and-a-half/three-year-old deciding to have a snack. They will know the routine of what is required. For example:

- first check if there is a space available at the snack table;

- select from the food on offer such as fruit, raisins, biscuit, cracker or a rice cake;

- select a drink and pour it into a glass;

- take the plate with the snack and the glass with the drink to the snack table;

- eat it while chatting to a friend;

- when finished, wash it all up, dry it; and

- dry their hands, ready to do something else.

This routine illustrates well how self-contained individual practical life activities contribute to the complex routine of having a snack and how much the child learns from every such routine and how a physical activity contributes to the holistic development of the child in the following ways:

- The sequence requires memory, problem solving and estimation when choosing the snack and drink, and when washing the dishes.

- The social interaction at the snack table contributes towards growing social awareness and communication skills. Often, two friends will decide to have a snack together and will be helpful to each other as well as have some fun while eating.

- When all is finished, imagine the sense of achievement for the three-year-old, who has managed it all by themselves including the washing up!

There are many examples of such complex routines in the Montessori classroom that build on the individual skills practised in the practical life area of the classroom.

Generally, the practical life activities are divided into three distinct groups (Gettman 1987):

1. exercises for refinement of movement – such as pouring, transferring, cutting, gluing, folding, opening and closing of boxes/bottles, and threading.

2. exercises for care of the environment – such as sweeping, polishing, dusting, washing and looking after plants, pets and the garden.

3. exercises for care of self that include activities and skills supporting personal independence – such as washing hands and blowing one's nose, as well activities promoting grace and courtesy – such as greeting visitors, offering a snack to a friend, and asking for help.

The practical life activities are often the first area of interest for the newcomer to a Montessori classroom because of their familiarity, relative simplicity and self-contained nature. However, as children become more competent, the skills acquired in this area will be used daily in supporting the organisation and maintenance of the classroom. They become the daily life of the classroom as children will offer to wipe tables after an activity, sweep up after lunch, wash the dishes or dirty polishing cloths. The activities take on social importance and give children opportunities to contribute to the well-being of the group, and in the process boost their self-esteem and reflect their responsibilities within the group – a positive illustration of the 'cohesion of the social unit' we have discussed in the previous chapter.

The practical life activities also often act as the 'secure base' (Bowlby 1988) for children, who may be worried or anxious; their simplicity will offer security and predictability as well as opportunities to be successful at achieving the chosen tasks. Whilst children carry on with their practical life activities, you will often overhear their monologues reflecting symbolic play (Piaget 1962). As they pour water from a jug to a glass, they are preparing a cup of tea for a friend, or medicine for their sick dolly. In this way, the activities act as a catalyst for spontaneous imaginative play, which usually takes place in the 'home corner' of mainstream settings.

It is important to add that just as these activities reflect everyday life, Montessori believed it was very important that they also reflect the culture of the children. Today's Montessori classrooms are often as international as the approach and so you may well observe the use of chopsticks, preparation of Arabic dishes, or re-enactment of a Japanese tea ceremony as well as the use of African beads in threading activities or making of bread for a harvest festival.

As part of this area of learning, you may encounter a game called 'Walking on the Line'. Fundamentally, this is a balancing game, focusing on following a line drawn on the floor. Children can make this game more challenging by walking on the line whilst carrying different objects such as a flag or a glass with water. This activity also offers challenges in negotiation if several children take part in the game at the same time.

Another game often played in Montessori classrooms is the 'Silence Game'. This game was inspired by a baby visiting a Montessori classroom.

The baby's stillness prompted Montessori to urge the children to listen to the stillness and quietness created, not only by everybody's adoration of the baby, but also by the baby herself. Montessori developed this activity further to encourage children in moments of stillness to be shared by the whole group. The 'Silence Game' gives children the opportunity to demonstrate their self-discipline during the shared moment of peace. This game is not played as a means of settling or calming a group of children. Only those children, who are mature enough to control their movements and have the necessary self-discipline will benefit from the social experience of the 'Silence Game'.

Refinement of the senses

Activities in this area of the classroom represent the early materials developed by Montessori. Some of these were inspired by the Froebel Gifts, such as the geometric solids, while others can be linked with Seguin and still others are Montessori's own inventions.

The main purpose of these activities is to help the child organise and classify the impressions of the environment gathered during earlier stages

of their life. Opportunities to use treasure baskets, engage with heuristic bags and explore nature all contribute to real experiences of the world, which are developed further whilst using the equipment and activities in this area of learning. Sensorial materials offer systematic refinement of the five senses as well as the child's stereognostic and kinaesthetic sense, which represent the exploration of three- and two-dimensional forms (in the Montessori context, the geometric solids such as cubes, prisms, cones, pyramids, and outlines of squares, circles, triangles respectively).

For Montessori, these materials hold the key to the understanding of fundamental concepts and the possibility of the expansion of the child's cognitive capabilities. The materials respond to the child's sensitive period for refinement of the senses (Montessori 1966), offer opportunities for manipulation and the extension of vocabulary and further exploration and application, beyond the realm of the Montessori classroom. With their frequent focus on matching, pairing, sorting and grading, they are also integral to building the foundation for mathematical understanding (Liebeck 1984).

- The activities for the refinement of the senses focus the child's attention and learning on each of their different senses:

- The visual sense: the child explores the properties and relationship of cubes, prisms, cylinders and rods, as well as the relationship of colours and their shades.

- The stereognostic sense: the child builds on the visual experiences of geometric forms as they explore the properties of the solid shapes by grouping them according to same/similar properties (such as whether or not a shape rolls), comparing them to the two-dimensional shapes of their bases and matching pairs of solid shapes. An activity in this area, which focuses on the tactile aspects, without using visual discrimination, is the mystery bag. This bag contains sets of matching objects; the child is expected to pair them by feel. The child also has an opportunity to learn about flat shapes, using both the visual and kinaesthetic senses. They explore them further as they come to work with the binomial and trinomial cubes. The knowledge of flat shapes is extended by giving children opportunities to make patterns.

- The tactile sense: the child explores varying textures of sandpapers, fabrics and papers. The child also has the opportunity to work with tablets of varying weight and temperature.

- The auditory sense: the child engages in a range of activities that heighten listening skills using sound boxes. In addition, the child is introduced to the basics of musical notation using the bells.

- Taste and smell: the child does activities involving food, including cooking, and learns about flowers, fruits and vegetables in cultural lessons.

The activities available in the sensorial area offer children keys to the universe (Montessori 1988a) – points of reference to key concepts such as shape, size and so on. They are organised in such a way as to support assimilation and accommodation of schemas, and so contribute towards concept formation through the manipulative nature of the activities. For Montessori, vocabulary expansion has a specific purpose in the context of these materials and in order to teach new vocabulary, the Montessori teacher uses a technique developed by Seguin called the three-period lesson.

The sequence in which we work with the sensorial materials focuses first on exploration of qualities, then on systematic identification of properties of the materials followed by vocabulary expansion that serves to 'polarise the child's attention', as Montessori (1988a) called it, and so to maximise the child's learning potential.

From the point of view of Montessori education today, the sensorial activities still form the foundation of later academic learning. It is also important to understand that like all foundations, the opportunity to extend the child's knowledge of these concepts and apply them to contexts that are familiar and meaningful to the child is very important. Through the application of these concepts in social context, we can see what the children learned and understood by using the sensorial materials. For example, it is important for Montessori teachers to offer opportunities for open-ended exploration of the qualities and properties of shapes by offering children opportunities to use unit blocks (Gura 1992). They can also make patterns using collage and drawing. We can also encourage immediate extensions of classroom learning into the outdoor environment by applying the tactile classroom experiences to finding rough and smooth surfaces in the garden or on a nature walk. Equally, outdoor experiences can be applied to activities available inside the classroom such as looking up a bug in a book or playing sound lotto, which relates to sounds from nature such as bird song or thunder. The older child can extend their knowledge of the Montessori bells and music notation to playing an instrument or being encouraged to compose original music.

Sensorial activities prepare children for academic learning later. It has been pointed out that by working with the geometric forms and other materials, the child learns to classify and organise information by matching, pairing and grading objects; this will be beneficial when exploring the one-to-one correspondence between quantities and symbols in mathematics, and when sequencing numerals. Many of the sensorial activities will also serve as beneficial preparation for other areas of learning, such as listening for small differentiations in sounds, which will tune the ear to listening out for letter sounds. The child will use visual, auditory and tactile experiences when they are introduced to sandpaper letters or numerals (as described on pp. 67 and 69), when letter/numeral shapes will be absorbed kinaesthetically, using all three senses as well as muscular memory.

The practical life and sensorial activities are usually offered to children from the age of two and will be the main focus of the children's learning in the Montessori nurseries in England where children usually enter into reception classes of primary schools soon after their fourth birthday.

Communication, language and literacy

Montessori was surprised by children's ability to learn to write and read much earlier than generally expected when she started to explore the possibilities in this area of learning. This was at the request of the parents whose children attended the first Children's House. It is important to understand and appreciate that introducing reading and writing in the Montessori classroom is possible because of the foundation laid in

the practical life and sensorial areas, but should only take place if the children show interest. The activities and materials such as insets for design and sandpaper letters should not be used as tools for accelerated learning. Listening to and engaging in conversations as well as hearing rich use of language are the essential stepping stones, which prepare children for later literacy activities.

Availability and use of a good range of books, and the increased phonological awareness of the child (achieved through games such as 'Odd Man Out' or simplified 'I Spy') play a crucial role in laying the foundation for learning to read and write. However, it is also important to remember that not all children will be ready or interested in being introduced to letters and writing in nursery; the key to identifying the child's readiness remains in the adult's observations and conversations with the child.

The journey towards reading and writing is often initially motivated by personal interest, such as recognition of one's own, a friend's or sibling's names. It is vital that we acknowledge that in the early years, this journey is likely to be longer and not as clearly defined as it is when the child is five, six or seven.

Ever since the early days, Montessorians have approached this area of

learning through phonics, focusing on letter sounds and shapes using the sandpaper letters. They provide a multi-sensory approach to absorption of the letter sounds and shapes by both visual and tactile means.

Children are prepared for use of writing implements early, both through the refinement of their fine motor movements within the practical life areas of the classroom and within the creative area. Their ability to control a pencil is further refined by the use of insets for design.

The child first learns to build words using cut-out letters (many children do this at home using magnetic letters to form their names and familiar words on the fridge) and by careful listening to letter sounds. They start by building words with predictable patterns of a single, short vowel placed between the two consonants, such as cat and mat. Use of 'onset and rime' (Lawrence 1998; MCI 2006) at this stage of learning serves as an important tool for the introduction of reading and so the decoding of words.

Further challenges are presented gradually by first introducing consonant blends such as pr- (pram), fr- (frog) and st- (stem, stamp), before words with more complex spelling are tackled. Each spelling difficulty is introduced through a series of reading and word-building activities, which help to memorise the new letter pattern. The child has the opportunity to work systematically through boxes, indentifying blends, diagraphs, trigraphs and phonograms. The individual boxes offer reading activities, whilst the word-building activities highlight spelling patterns. Further reading opportunities are available in word lists, phrase and sentence strips, and reading books, accompanying the different levels of complexity, supporting growing reading skills.

In the Montessori classroom, children are also introduced to grammar using colour-coding for parts of speech and building sentences with the help of objects. These activities offer sensorial introduction to grammar and also serve as extra reading opportunities.

Wherever possible, we offer the child objects that can be manipulated in order to both prompt and scaffold the child's learning. As explained previously, due to the early age at which children leave Montessori nurseries in England, it is the phonological awareness and general pre-reading activities such as storytelling, using books with props or sequencing of stories that prepare children for more systematic literacy work in primary schools.

Numeracy and arithmetic

Children often come to nursery with a passive knowledge of numbers through everyday use, such as counting steps, reciting nursery rhymes, looking at number books and recognising numerals on car number plates or on houses. They may also have the ability, for example, to count the three candles on a birthday cake and recognise the numeral on a birthday card. Initially children are introduced to concepts such as matching, pairing and sorting, and to shapes and patterns in the sensorial area of the classroom. These concepts prepare them for later work in mathematics.

The Montessori numeracy and arithmetic materials offer a systematic approach to learning about the integrity of numbers in relation to numerals, always using objects to support the learning. The golden bead materials, designed to introduce children to the hierarchies of the decimal system while exploring the place value using both the beads and the written symbols of the large number cards, are probably the most unique

and original contribution made by Montessori to learning mathematics. They give the child the opportunity to explore the relationships between the hierarchies of the decimal system before the child is presented with addition and subtraction of units.

All activities within the nursery mathematics syllabus are presented to the child through the use of objects while gradually building an understanding of numbers. The tools for introduction of operations such as addition, subtraction, multiplication and division are also available to Montessori teachers working with children up to the age of six. They are rarely used in Montessori nurseries in England due to the children's early school leaving age.

Montessori classrooms also give children opportunities to use number knowledge in everyday contexts and within contexts meaningful to the child, such as counting how many biscuits will be needed for a snack or recognising numerals on a birthday chart. Number books are available and children often play number games in the garden or playground while cooking and gardening, and these serve as meaningful tools for the application of counting skills in the daily life of the classroom. The role-play area is another place where children use number knowledge spontaneously and with great eloquence.

Cultural aspects of life

This area of the classroom has the least prescribed materials. It offers opportunities for children and teachers to explore a wide range of topics of interest in biology, geography and history. The activities in this area should centre on real experiences that give children opportunities to observe, explore and investigate such things as trees, seasons, farmyard animals, the solar system, how a volcano works and so on.

In the areas of natural sciences such as botany and zoology, we start by observing and becoming familiar with the immediate environment within the child's community. We work from the opposite perspective in geography, embracing the whole solar system and exploring the natural aspects of global physical geography before looking at the continents and countries where we live.

The nature/project table is often used as the focus for this area of learning. A range of teacher-made materials complement the child's initial real experiences. These materials support and develop the child's language and literacy skills and encourage the child's individual learning by using primarily matching and pairing teaching strategies.

Like most of the materials in the Montessori classroom, cultural activities are designed to be used by individual children or small groups, supported where appropriate by an adult. Very few of these materials are suitable for large group teaching. Most of the activities in this area of learning should be planned with the children and built on their interest, rather than determined by adult perceptions of what the child should learn.

History is explored through time lines and natural cycles that help children understand the passage of time, a concept alien to most children. This is seen as preparation for later and more systematic study of natural history from an evolutionary perspective.

The exploration of continents and their countries also gives us opportunities to explore similarities and differences in the lives of children and their families around the world. Montessori saw these activities as important learning tools in developing children's understanding of and respect for all humanity as a foundation towards peaceful co-existence. Peace education continues to be a key aspect of the spiritual development of the child in the Montessori classroom and is extensively enlarged upon in the Montessori primary curriculum through the concept of cosmic education (Montessori 1989d, 1994; Montessori Jnr 1992).

For Montessori, cosmic education represents not only the idea that each one of us is part of the larger cosmos, but also that we are in a state of constant change or evolution. Nothing is static in the universe, and all living as well as not-living aspects of our existence are interconnected and interdependent on each other. This inter-relationship places a great responsibility on each one of us. We are all part of this universal link and our individual actions and behaviours ultimately impact on the existence of all humanity.

Creativity

This area of learning acknowledges the importance of self-expression and highlights the need for children to have opportunities to participate in self-chosen and self-initiated arts and craft activities, as well as music and movement and socio-dramatic play.

A well-equipped Montessori nursery has an area of the classroom where children have all the necessary resources freely available to paint, using both an easel and watercolours. Children are also given the opportunity to draw using a range of good quality tools such a crayons, coloured pencils and felt tips as well as a variety of different kinds of paper. They also have resources to glue and make collages, and to print using stamps as well as natural resources such as vegetables, wood or sponge stamps. Teachers help children to develop skills necessary for the activities, such as how to apply glue or use scissors, but the activities themselves are open-ended and offer endless possibilities for self-expression.

Musical instruments, particularly percussion instruments, are also available for spontaneous use, and teachers sing regularly with the

children. Specialist music teachers may join the children regularly to sing and initiate music and movement activities.

Storytelling, as well as story time using books and props, is common-place in Montessori classrooms. This often happens spontaneously when a child asks for a story, and usually a small group gathers around the adult in the book area of the classroom. Some nurseries also have story time for the whole group at the end of the day. All these activities can be incorporated into the spontaneous, choice-led work cycle and do not require all children to stop what they are doing in order to participate.

Many of these activities happen inside the classroom, but there are also opportunities for these activities to be conducted outside. You may also see a Montessori teacher dramatising stories for children to act out. What you may not see is a role-play area using a wide range of props that has been set up by adults on a particular theme, such as a shop or a post office. Much of the role play in Montessori classrooms is spontaneous, inspired by clothes from around the world or emerging from the variety of topics studied in the classroom, such as visits to the seaside or the zoo or, as previously mentioned, emerging from work in the practical life area of the classroom. As with all role play, the best role-play scenarios emerge spontaneously when children use their imagination to create their props and when adults support their creativity sensitively without much intrusion.

See Appendix 2 for detailed lists of Montessori learning materials, which can be found in the areas of learning of a Montessori nursery.

Montessori practice and the Early Years Foundation Stage

Exploration of the principles and their reflection in statutory guidance

Having examined the Montessori approach, this chapter will explain links between the Early Years Foundation Stage (May 2008) and Montessori early years practice. It will reflect on the principles, which underpin both approaches and make links with the statutory guidance.

The principled approach

When the Early Years Foundation Stage (EYFS) document was first published in 2007, it highlighted the need for establishing robust principles to underpin early years practice. Four key strands were identified, each comprising four aspects. They are: The Unique Child, Enabling Environments, Positive Relationships, and Learning and Development. They reflect the current agenda for children as expressed both in the *United Nations Convention on the Rights of the Child* (UN 1989) and the UK's aspirational green paper, *Every Child Matters* (2002). They also reflect Montessori's aim of *'following the child'*, as described in the previous chapters, by highlighting the close relations between the child, the teacher and the favourable environment in supporting children's learning and development.

The then Department for Education and Skills presented practitioners with an overarching document, combining a regulatory framework as previously included in Ofsted's National Standards together with guidance for learning and development of children from birth to the end of the reception year. This ambitious plan is intended to streamline procedures and to link all agencies, parents and practitioners working with young children by use of one framework – from childminders to managers of children centres and head teachers in primary schools. Whilst this 'one-size-fits-all' approach has not been without its problems, the principled approach has been recognised as an essential component of high-quality early years practice and has been welcomed by all working with young children.

The Montessori community were given an opportunity to reflect on their practice in relation to the Early Years Foundation Stage by producing 'Guide to the Early Years Foundation Stage in Montessori Settings'. This document, funded by the Department for Children, Schools and Families, was produced by the National Strategies and Montessori Schools Association, and published early in 2008 by the Montessori Schools Association (MSA). It is available from the Montessori St Nicholas Charity both electronically and in paper format and also electronically from the National Strategies website.

The four principles, as expressed in the sixteen strands, challenge practitioners to reflect on their practice and ensure that they are embedded in every aspect of their practice in support of the care and education they provide for children attending their settings. So let us examine how they relate to the Montessori approach of *'following the child'* where respectful and trusting adults support children's learning by preparing an environment favourable for their development. *'Following the child'* also means that practitioners understand that children are active learners, have inner lives, which are evident in their inner motivation and therefore flourish in an atmosphere of freedom. This freedom within limits guides children towards self-regulation as demonstrated by self-discipline. The deep respect for the child is reflected in the pedagogy, which is built on access to a favourable environment prepared to meet the individual child's needs and facilitation of learning by empathetic and knowledgeable practitioners.

The unique child

Every child is a competent learner from birth, who can be resilient, capable, confident and self-assured.

The four aspects identified as essential in supporting the characteristics of the unique child are:

1. knowledge of child development

2. inclusive practice

3. keeping safe

4. health and well-being.

From the Montessori perspective, these aspects are interpreted as follows:

- *Children's development* is identified in three distinct and unique stages, which are described in Chapter 2. Children's sensitive periods are used as a guide for identification of areas of interest and then reflected in the child's learning. Montessori teachers are also introduced to developmental theories and should be able to interpret children's behaviours from both perspectives. They should use their knowledge and understanding of the individual children, based on regular observation, for planning of further learning and to adjust the favourable environment to meet their individual needs.

- *Inclusive practice* is reflected in both the setting's policies as required by the Statutory Framework and by the practitioners' recognition of the uniqueness of each child, whose family and community are valued and respected. Furthermore, full access to all services provided by the setting is given to all the children attending.

- *Keeping safe* recognises that children are vulnerable and adults have the responsibility to protect them, so that they are able to develop their potential. All Montessori providers ensure that they meet all aspects of the safeguarding requirements as identified in the Statutory Framework. In addition, Montessori practitioners also give children opportunities to use their initiative and take risks, within well-established risk assessment procedures.

- *Health and well-being* are at the core of Montessori practice by helping children to establish positive attitudes to healthy eating and ensuring that children's physical and psychological needs are met in support of their well-being. This relates to daily routines, children's freedom within the classroom, both inside and outside, as well as respect and trust modelled by adults and peers.

Positive relationships: children learn to be strong and independent from a base of loving and secure relationships with parents and/or a key person

The four aspects identified as essential in supporting the characteristics of positive relationships are:

1. respecting each other

2. parents as partners

3. supporting learning

4. key person.

From the Montessori perspective, these aspects are interpreted as follows:

- It should be evident from all that has been written so far about the Montessori approach that it is firmly rooted in *mutual respect* and trust in the child, which are modelled by the adults and older children. It should be reflected in all relationships where children are trusted to be the leaders of their own learning as supported by the favourable environment. Children are also encouraged to think of themselves as 'citizens of the world', particularly when engaging in activities and with materials which develop their knowledge and understanding of the world. The vertical grouping (organised in three-year age spans, according to the stage of development discussed in Chapter 2) in

Montessori settings further promotes the mutual respect between children of different ages and contributes significantly towards positive relationships.

● Montessori recognised that children thrive when parents and the setting co-operate in supporting the child. *Parents as partners* have been integral to good Montessori practice for many years, with parents participating in the activities within the settings and owners and managers offering regular opportunities for parents to learn more about their philosophy and practice.

● Key to Montessori pedagogy is the notion of individual development, therefore, for many years it has been Montessori practice to plan for each child. Individual learning plans relating to Montessori areas of learning support children in their unique development, building on their interest and *supporting learning* as and where appropriate. This approach relates to all children in the setting, not just those with additional needs.

● The *key person* approach has been adopted by the majority of Montessori settings. Whilst the key person's unique responsibilities in relation to children and their families are recognised, in Montessori environments, all practitioners and adults are likely to contribute to the children's learning and record-keeping, without undermining the role of the key person. Modelling positive teamwork and respectful relationships within the group promotes a harmonious and calm learning environment.

Enabling environments: the environment plays a key role in supporting and extending children's development and learning

● observation, assessment and planning;

● supporting every child;

● the learning environment;

● the wider context.

From the Montessori perspective, we need to begin by examining the learning environment before the other three aspects are interpreted.

* *Observation* has been at the heart of Montessori practice for the past hundred years and serves as the main tool for *assessing* children's progress and *planning* for next steps. Further explanation of how observations support planning in Montessori classrooms can be found in Chapter 5 where children's learning and development are discussed in more detail.

* *Supporting every child* is how Montessori classrooms work because the emphasis is on individual progress and in the recognition of children's uniqueness. The organisation and accessibility of all learning further supports opportunities for independent learning and individual progress whilst being facilitated by a sensitive and knowledgeable adult.

* *The learning environment* is described in some detail in Chapters 2 and 3 where its role in support of spontaneous learning is highlighted. It is important to mention that many settings add to the activities and occupations, which are part of the Montessori legacy. However, these activities should be in keeping with the principles of the Montessori pedagogy. Since the 1950s, we have seen expansion of the creative areas of the Montessori environments and children will find high-quality resources for self-expression in a range of art media, collage, modelling, printing, mark-making as well as props for spontaneous role-play. The outdoor classroom concept should be well-embedded in Montessori practice, as should be activities such as gardening and care of pets, which were seen by Montessori (1988b) as essential in bringing children close to nature. Programmable toys and computers have become part of Montessori classrooms too, but generally they would be evident in environments providing for the older children – five, six and seven-year-olds. For the younger children, the focus is on providing real experiences, which enhance sensory learning and give children opportunities for learning about their environment. These experiences are seen by the Montessori teacher as fundamental in giving children a firm foundation for all future learning. The nature of

children's autonomous learning is supported by effective classroom management where practitioners ensure that cycles of activity are observed within the work-cycle and where children's play and work are the key tools for learning, whilst they explore the full range of the learning resources within the continuous provision of the classroom.

● Children in Montessori classrooms are encouraged to see themselves as 'citizens of the world' and experience both the immediate community in which they are growing up and also the global community. Therefore, their experiences of the *wider context* of the enabling environment are rich and link with cross-cultural experiences and growing respect for our planet and all life within it.

Before examining learning and development in Montessori classrooms, it is vital to point out that the three principles and their aspects discussed above have to be embedded in the classroom practice as essential components of quality, if highly meaningful learning and development is to take place.

Montessori practice and the Early Years Foundation Stage

Exploration of learning and development

The aim of this chapter is to explore how learning and development are delivered in Montessori classrooms and how they integrate with the Early Years Foundation Stage. For this purpose, activities offered to children across the full age-span of the EYFS will be discussed.

Learning and development is defined by the EYFS by the following statement

Children develop and learn in different ways and at different rates; and all areas of learning and development are equally important and integrated. This is exactly how Montessori practitioners view children's learning. Therefore, all planning is based on developmentally appropriate activities, which reflect the child's interest and promote engagement, concentration and exploration.

The EYFS identifies *play and exploration* as the key tool for effective learning. Montessori's perspective of play and learning has been discussed in Chapter 2 where the *active nature of children learning* is also addressed. Montessori is one of the pioneers of early years education, who identified young children's needs to 'learn by doing' or, as she called it, by manipulation. The spontaneous nature of children's learning in Montessori settings is supported by the organisation of the learning environment. The favourable environment, which is rich in learning opportunities based on play and exploration, naturally supports children's *critical thinking and creativity.* It provides children with time to play and discover. Montessorians view the child's creativity as 'a way of thinking', and it should be evident in all areas of learning and should be encouraged by practitioners at every opportunity.

The accessibility and organisation of activities according to areas of learning provide *planning tools* for the teacher and a guide for the child. These activities are described in detail in Montessori folders, which are compiled by Montessori students during their studies. They are a comprehensive set of lesson plans relating to many of the activities included in the classroom. As such, they serve as Montessori *schemes of work.* Each child's progress is recorded in the *individual learning plan,* which lists the progression of activities on offer, building on skills learned in small manageable steps. This organisation of children's learning scaffolds their progress. The child's individual learning plan is supplemented by detailed observations, samples of the child's work and photographs documenting their progress. All these records are part of the *child's learning journey,* which is shared with parents and children on a regular basis. They in turn are given opportunities to contribute to the document. All the records gathered by the practitioners, children and their families contribute to the formative assessment and, as such, are the evidence for the completion of the *Foundation Stage Profile* for those children, who stay in the Montessori setting until the summer term of the academic year in which they turn five. This statutory assessment tool to measure effectiveness of the early years provision is the 'bone of contention' for many Montessorians, who find it inappropriate for young children, attending non-compulsory education, to be subjected to assessment of this kind and to contribute to government statistical data.

Montessori early years curriculum explained in relation to the six areas of learning

● personal, social and emotional development;

● communication, language and literacy;

- problem solving, reasoning and numeracy;
- knowledge and understanding of the world;
- physical development;
- creative development.

Personal, social and emotional development

When exploring the aspects of this area of learning, we find that the ground rules as well as the opportunities to work with the activities for an extended period of time support children's *dispositions and attitudes*. The teachers and older children model attitudes of kindness, politeness as well as perseverance and diligence and consistency.

Self-confidence and self-esteem are nurtured by the independence gained from perfecting skills such as pouring, transferring, learning to do up buttons and buckles, helping look after animals and plants in the classroom and in the garden. As children grow more competent in what they do, they are able to support every aspect of daily routine in the classroom, sometimes on their own and at other times with the help of friends and adults.

This participation contributes towards establishing *relationships* with their teachers. Peer friendships and co-operation are extended as children settle into the classroom and learn to take turns by returning materials back to the shelves, or share in activities such as preparation for lunch or gardening.

Ground rules as well as role models provided by the teachers and older children *encourage positive behaviour and self-control*, which evolve from the freedoms offered by the classroom and from the responsibility that comes with this freedom – such as being able to choose what to do, but knowing that the activity has to be returned back to the shelf, ready for another child to use. Courteous behaviour is modelled and encouraged at all times.

The practical life area is organised into three groups, and the area for 'care of self', where children learn to wash their hands, put on shoes and clothes when going outside or returning home or brushing their teeth after meals, contributes directly to the *self-care* of all children in the setting.

The fact that the child is able to contribute towards the daily organisation and routines of classroom life makes a major contribution to their sense of belonging and therefore *sense of community*. Through celebrations of festivals and culturally appropriate practical life activities, such as learning to put on a kimono, setting table for Chinese lunch or giving thanks at harvest festival, children extend their sense of community beyond the boundaries of their immediate and familiar environment.

Communication, language and literacy

In this area of learning, there are six key features, which focus on communication as well as use of language as a cognitive skill and the introduction of reading and writing.

Montessori wrote extensively in *The Absorbent Mind* of the importance of language development and the role adults play in developing communication skills. The Montessori classroom encourages conversation, discussion and dialogue as part of everyday life. *Language for communication* is evident in every aspect of learning – during small group time, in group activities when games are played or science experiments carried out, when children work in pairs or alone and, as monologues are often overheard, as children verbalise what they are doing.

Language for thinking is encouraged by extending children's vocabulary through three-period lessons, so that children have the opportunities to express themselves using appropriate language. Children are also encouraged to talk about their work and ask questions to help them in problem solving and exploration of materials. Storybooks play an important role in extending children's communication skills by offering rich and imaginative use of language. Information books support children's thinking and memory. Teachers and children verbalise their thoughts, and use and model language for thinking whilst they are working with Montessori materials and activities.

Montessori teachers approach *reading and writing* simultaneously and base their lessons on the *phonic approach* (Montessori 1988b). The multi-sensory benefits of the sandpaper letters give children opportunities to be introduced both to the letter shape and sound as they hear the sound of the individual letters while they trace their shape outlined in sandpaper. There can be no more effective way of linking the two together.

However, much work has to be done in order to develop children's phonic awareness prior to introducing the sandpaper letters. Games such as 'I Spy' and 'Odd Man Out' contribute greatly to children's awareness of letter sounds and give them the opportunity to link letter sound with initial sounds in their names and in words. Rhymes, poems and stories further contribute towards the child's awareness of letters and their sounds.

Linking sounds and letters is introduced simultaneously and children are prepared for writing, long before we introduce them to the insets for design, the materials specifically developed by Montessori to help control of pencil, lightness of touch and directionality of writing. The majority of practical life and sensorial exercises develop manipulative skills and focus on the dynamic tripod grip and develop the hand muscles and flexible wrist in preparation for writing.

In addition, children in Montessori classrooms benefit from easily accessible writing implements that are usually available alongside the inset for design or in the art area of the classroom. Accessibility of painting at an easel cannot be underestimated as an important contribution to the development of arm movement and gross motor skills required prior to developing the smaller muscles, supporting the use of writing implements. Children are also encouraged to *'write without writing'*, using their knowledge of letter sounds and letter shapes to formulate words with the large movable alphabet.

As awareness has grown in the importance of cursive letter shapes, many Montessori nursery schools have been using the Sassoon cursive alphabet for their sandpaper letters, so encouraging appropriate letter formation and focusing on the exit strokes used in joined-up *handwriting*. This gives children an excellent preparation for the more formal lessons in handwriting that they will receive in primary schools.

Reading is introduced in a three-tier approach, focusing first on three-letter words consisting of 'consonant, vowel, consonant' words such as 'cat' at the beginning level. Children utilise their knowledge of letters and are prepared for blending of sounds into words by word-building and 'onset and rime' activities.

Initially, children 'read words' and use objects to match to word cards they have read. Gradually, as they get more practice decoding words, they use fewer props and move from single words to reading phrases, sentences and books. Many of the children attending Montessori settings in England do not benefit from the activities described below because they are designed for older children.

The same progression is followed at the second level when children tackle initial and final blends such as pr- in pram or -lt in kilt. Double consonants, as in carrot or bonnet, and -ck as in lock or rock, are introduced next, and most common digraphs such as sh- in shell, ch- in chips and th- in thin feature next.

These prepare children for the third stage of reading when individual phonograms are studied, first by reading and then by focusing on the spelling patterns in words like barn (b-ar-n). Before children progress onto the third reading level, they also study grammar, and colour-coding is used to introduce parts of speech.

These early grammar activities not only introduce parts of speech, but also give children further opportunities to practise their reading. Unfortunately, as most children in England leave Montessori nursery schools around the age of four, they seldom benefit from the full range of reading activities available to children in the rest of the world, who usually attend Montessori schools until the age of six.

Problem solving, reasoning and numeracy

The preparation for mathematics that children receive in Montessori settings starts in the sensorial area as children refine their senses by exploring shape, pattern and weight. These activities introduce concepts of one-to-one correspondence (knobbed cylinders), seriation (the pink tower, the broad stair, long rods and coloured cylinders), sorting (constructive triangles) and so on.

Mathematical concepts are experienced and absorbed by children long before they are introduced to mathematics in a formal way. This is one of the reasons why Montessori (1988a) refers to the sensorial materials as 'materialised abstractions'. Children in Montessori classrooms have the opportunity to be introduced to mathematical language in the context of everyday life, such as when getting ready to go outside, having snacks, during cooking sessions, and in the art and book areas.

The Montessori mathematical curriculum focuses primarily on numbers and the relationships between quantities and written symbols. A range of materials help children understand the unique relationship between *numbers as labels and for counting*. The materials highlight the one-to-one correspondence between quantity and symbol as children use number rods and cards, the spindle box, and cards and counters. This foundation to the number base of ten is further explored when children are introduced to the hierarchies of the decimal system. They use the golden bead material and colour-coded numeral cards and materials for counting up to 100. The patterns created by table exercises are explored by the older children, as are fractions.

Once children have secure knowledge of numbers to ten, they will be also introduced to number operations using a range of activities, such as the group operations with the golden beads, the snake game, number rods, short bead stair and strip boards. *Calculating* using objects and gradually recording the answers is a natural progression from the activities for counting to ten. It also complements the spontaneous calculation opportunities present in the everyday life of the classroom – during cooking, when using play-dough, and when working with the sensorial materials and unit blocks.

The sensorial area of learning provides many opportunities for problem-solving, reasoning and also for exploration of *shape and space*. Children use the geometric solids and their three-dimensional qualities, and the geometric cabinet to become familiar with flat shapes. Gradually they become aware of the relationship between the solid and flat shapes. Naming shapes such as prisms, cuboids, cylinders, pyramids, rectangles, hexagons and parallelograms become part of everyday life of the classroom. The flat and solid shapes give many opportunities to explore spatial relationships and patterns.

Measurement is primarily introduced during cooking activities. We also use the longest (1 metre/100 centimetres) or shortest (10 centimetres) red rods from the sensorial area as a unit of measurement, particularly when considering height and length.

Knowledge and understanding of the world

This area of learning corresponds directly to what is called in the Montessori classroom the cultural area. The activities in this area focus on biology, geography, history and science. Here, the Montessori early years curriculum consists of a range of teacher-made materials, often developed in conjunction with topics or projects introduced to the classroom. These topics and projects are often negotiated with the children and should reflect the children's interests and fascinations. The focus is, whenever possible, on real experiences that enhance and complement learning through the senses, so appropriate for this age group.

All Montessori classrooms should have plants and flowers both inside and outside in the garden. They are often part of the nature table that reflects 'finds and discoveries' during nature walks and from the garden. They also give opportunities for children to bring items into the classroom that they have found during walks with their parents or on the way to school – such as conkers, leaves, snails and so on. The nature table serves as a focus for *observation, exploration and investigation.* Real experiences are complemented by access to books, pictures and teacher-made materials. The nature table usually reflects the topics or projects and may relate to work on transport, my body, minibeasts, volcanoes, continents, solar system as well as more abstract themes such as electricity, magnetism or light.

The sense of *time* is introduced with the help of a range of time lines and life cycles, and by regular use of calendars. Birthdays are celebrated and also contribute to the children's understanding of the passage of time.

Learning about *places* is approached from a unique perspective in Montessori classrooms as the child becomes aware of the solar system and the planet Earth and its continents, long before they come to study the country in which they were born. This is part of the Montessori ethos and focuses on giving children the opportunity of becoming 'citizens of the world'.

Montessori teachers introduce continents from a multi-sensory perspective, first by looking at the globe and then by working with the puzzle map of the world that identifies each continent by its unique colour. Collections of objects and pictures from each continent are contained within artefact boxes and give children opportunities to explore each continent through its music, clothes, food, plants and animals as well as festivals and geographical features. The boxes are fundamental in bringing the lives and *cultures and communities* of different continents into the classroom and, by doing so, promoting multi-cultural awareness and respect.

Designing and making skills are developed and encouraged through activities such as carpentry and craft and other activities in the practical life area. In this aspect of learning, Montessori teachers observe children, discuss their ideas and make resources available to ensure that children have opportunities to develop their design ideas.

There are many Montessori classrooms that include a computer as part of their resources available to the children within the aspect of *information and communication technology*. However, debate continues within the Montessori community as to the value of computers, particularly if they take over from the real experiences of life.

For example, the experience of feeling the texture of a leaf or shell, smelling a flower, or feeling the wetness of a snail slithering along the arm cannot be replaced by seeing computer images. On the other hand, the children have everyday technology available to them in the practical life area, such as scales, a grinder and graters, sticky tape dispenser, telephones, tape recorders and digital cameras. If these are available they are functioning objects rather than models or replicas. Many Montessori classrooms have also invested in a range of programmable toys.

Physical development

Physical development is inherent in all the activities carried out in the Montessori classroom. Small children learn by doing and, therefore, manipulation is a key strategy for learning.

Movement consists of gross and fine motor skills, awareness of *space* and balance. These are part of the daily life of the Montessori classroom; children choose activities, carry them to their chosen space, engage with them and put them away. They need to plan where they want to do their chosen activities and have to negotiate the space available to them. Once settled in their space, either on the floor or at a table, they have the opportunity to repeat an activity and perfect the given skill. Montessori saw very close links between motor skills and brain development, calling the hand the 'instrument of man's intelligence' (Montessori 1988a: 127). Manipulation and refinement of movement is encouraged by the use of a range of equipment, tools and materials.

Here, we have the opportunity to make cross-curricular links primarily between physical and creative development, and knowledge and understanding of the world. From the Montessori point of view, all the Montessori curriculum areas contribute to the refinement of the child's movement with special and unique contribution made by both practical life and sensorial areas. This learning may take place indoors as well as outdoors as Montessori was a great advocate of outdoor learning and recognised the importance of what we call today the outdoor classroom. Music and movement activities also contribute to this area of learning. Children have many opportunities to use a wide range of *equipment and materials*, which promote all aspects of physical development

Health and bodily awareness are once again part of everyday activities within the classroom as they become part of the daily routine, particularly during meal times and outdoor activities. Special projects devoted to 'my body' or 'myself' will also reflect this aspect of the early years foundation curriculum. Many Montessori settings are committed to healthy-eating programmes and regulate the food offered to children by the nursery or brought into the nursery from home.

Creative development

Creativity provides children with opportunities to develop both their physical skills as well as their imagination. This area of learning in the Montessori classrooms has come under criticism in the past, but current training of Montessori teachers has addressed this component of the curriculum. The emphasis on creativity helps children develop skill in using resources spontaneously and gives opportunities for development of the imagination, with support from the adults in the classroom.

This area of development has significant links with the practical life and in the sensorial area, particularly if we understand the child's creativity to be the ability to use their imagination. Children are given opportunities to *respond in a variety of ways to what they see, hear, smell, touch and feel.*

Children are given many *opportunities to explore colour, texture, shape, form and space in two and three dimensions* within the art area of the classroom where resources are readily available and accessible and offer many opportunities for spontaneous learning. Children engage in painting, drawing using a variety of resources, collage, printing, modelling exploring a range of materials from play-dough to clay, as well as boxes, tubes, containers.

Opportunities to express and communicate ideas relate to use of arts and crafts materials, musical instruments and drama props, such as puppets and objects from story sacks. All are available in Montessori classrooms and usually children have the opportunity to access them during the three-hour work cycle rather than during organised lessons. However, in addition to the spontaneous use, some nurseries also employ a specialist teacher, who gives more formal lessons once a week in the areas of their expertise such as music, art, craft or drama.

Singing is part of the daily routine of Montessori classrooms, and musical instruments are also available, usually under supervision of the teacher. Movement often becomes an integral part of the music lessons as children act out songs and demonstrate specific movement; usually this is the first introduction to drama. Children also have opportunities to listen to a variety of music, such as music from different continents, folk, jazz or classical music. These activities give children the opportunity to *recognise and explore patterns in music, how sounds can be changed and how to match movements to music.*

It is not very common to see role-play areas designed by teachers in the Montessori classrooms. This does not mean that children are not given the opportunity to develop their imagination, but it is more likely that role-play scenarios will evolve spontaneously and will reflect the children's own experiences of life. This approach relies on the adults' observation skills and good range of resources to facilitate role play as it emerges. The adult involvement is essential if opportunities to facilitate children's use of imagination are not to be missed.

In a way, all that happens in the classroom requires the opportunity for children and adults to be engaged in a dialogue. Children need to be given time to express and communicate their ideas in a chosen medium, be it painting, drawing, modelling, carpentry, blocks, dance, singing and playing an instrument, role play or gardening. Creativity is present in all that children do in the classroom *promoting their imagination in art and design, stories, music, dance, imaginative and role-play.*

See Appendix 1 for an example of how a Montessori nursery may meet the early learning goals. Many Montessori nurseries develop similar grids that they share with parents to demonstrate how their setting meets the criteria of the EYFS and to explain their planning and record-keeping systems. They also find it helpful when explaining their practice to Ofsted inspectors and other visitors to her setting such as advisors from the local authority.

6
Montessori practice in the United Kingdom today

Montessori is a global movement with children's houses and primary schools in over 100 countries around the world. The centenary celebrations in 2007 gave Montessorians in all parts of the globe an opportunity to raise awareness of the relevance of Montessori education to lives of children in the twenty-first century. The aim of this chapter is to look at Montessori education in the United Kingdom, and particularly in England, where the majority of Montessori provision and training can be found at present.

During the past ten years we have seen a growing interest in Montessori education in this country. Some of it coincides with the increasing political focus on early years, which is linked to funding for pre-school education first initiated in 1995 with the voucher scheme. Some of it is due to the efforts of the Montessori St Nicholas Charity who are investing in promotion of the Montessori approach with three major initiatives. First, they established the Montessori Schools Association in 2002 to give the community a voice; today 604 schools in the UK participate in the scheme and the MSA has two and half thousand individual members. The current growing interest in Montessori education by the maintained sector relates to the emergence of foundation units within many primary schools where the Montessori approach can be applied and successfully linked with the EYFS. To date the charity has supported four primary schools by providing them with financial help as well as training and mentoring opportunities. The other significant initiative funded by the St Nicholas trust is the accreditation scheme for Montessori schools launched in 2008. The charity also owns Montessori Centre International, a Montessori teacher training college, which offers a range of courses in this country and abroad.

Traditionally England is the place where Montessori teacher training has been attracting potential students from all over the world, and it remains so today. It is possible to study for a Montessori diploma, recognised by the Children's Workforce and Development Council as a level 4 qualification for working with young children. The diploma is offered by full time, part time and by distance learning study and offers theoretical and practical training relevant to working with young children following the Montessori approach. The UK government's aspirations to have a graduate leader in every early years setting by 2015 has resulted in many Montessori diploma holders embarking on further studies achieving early years degrees and the early years professional status. Montessori-based Foundation degrees have been validated by higher education establishments such as London Metropolitan University who is working in partnership with Montessori Centre International (MCI). The central London based MCI also offers professional development workshops and seminars for practising Montessorians. The Montessori St Nicholas Charity with MCI as its training arm ensures that Montessori schools are staffed with qualified Montessori teachers, who are prepared for work with young children in the twenty-first century.

The annual census (MSA 2009) conducted by the Montessori Schools Association under the leadership of Dr Martin Bradley revealed some interesting data about Montessori nurseries and schools in the UK. For example:

- Of the Montessori settings inspected by Ofsted, 88 per cent were graded at 'Outstanding' or 'Good' in their last inspection. The remaining 12 per cent graded as 'Satisfactory' or 'Satisfactory/Good'. This represents a high level of quality provision offered to the estimated 31,000 children in Montessori nurseries and schools.

- The size of the settings varies greatly from those set up in the proprietor's home attended by 5 children to purpose-built schools supporting up to 240 children.

- Sixty per cent of Montessori settings offer full time provision, whilst 40 per cent are sessional, often operating from community halls where they are required to set up their classroom every day, because they are using shared premises.

- Eleven per cent of the children attending, some 1,700, are between the ages of three months and two. The majority of children, over 13,000, attending Montessori provision are between the ages of two and five and just under 1000 children benefit from Montessori primary education.

- Of the 55 per cent of schools that responded to the census, 42 per cent were staffed by Montessori qualified teachers whist 58 per cent of the staff held other relevant early years qualifications or are not qualified. Of the qualified staff just under 2,000 hold a level 4 or higher qualifications, about 2,500 are qualified at level 3, whilst approximately 1,500 are level 2 qualified.

The quality of Montessori provision is of paramount importance. The 2008 established accreditation scheme offered by the Montessori Evaluation and Accreditation Board (MEAB) under the auspices of the Montessori St Nicholas Charity gives settings an opportunity to reflect on their provision in context of Montessori principles and those of the EYFS. They are assessed in a three-year cycle by appropriately trained and Montessori qualified assessors. The nurseries and schools who receive MEAB accreditation are indentified on the MSA database of schools which is linked with the full report available on the MEAB website (www.montessori. org.uk). This quality assurance scheme is supported by MCI professional development programme available and delivered either in individual settings or at the London-based Montessori Centre International. Since summer of 2008, 65 schools have been accredited and a further 50 are on the waiting list to be visited during 2009/2010 academic year. MEAB accredited settings are used by MCI as the preferred nurseries for placement of students for teaching practice.

The Charity's state school primary initiative, which was launched in 2005 at Gorton Mount Primary School in Manchester has brought Montessori education into the mainstream. Stebbing Primary School, at

Stebbing, Essex, Carleton St Hilda's Primary School, Carleton, Lancashire and Spitalgate Primary School in Grantham also participate in this initiative and have witnessed benefits not only for the children and their families but also for the staff in their schools.

At the foundation stage the Montessori approach offers children an opportunity to exercise their independence and to establish motivation within the classroom's favourable environment. The freedom within limits, the calm atmosphere and respectful attitudes promote self-esteem and self-respect and are reflected in the foundation profile scores of all the schools involved in the project particularly in the areas of personal, social and emotional development, problem solving, reasoning and numeracy and in creative development.

At Gorton we have seen gradual expansion of the Montessori approach from nursery and reception to years 1 and 2. The school has a long-term plan for continuous training of staff and in September 2009 established a Montessori training base, supported by the teachers who also received trainers training.

They are also exploring ways of introducing the Montessori approach in the junior school during the next couple of years.

It is rewarding to see that with the financial support from the charity and with forward-looking leadership and determination from the school staff and the head teachers, Montessori education is returning to its roots – offering the best to children as their full entitlement for free, high quality education.

Appendix 1

How the early learning goals are met at a Montessori nursery

This Appendix makes links between the Early Learning Goals and Montessori practice. This is not a finite list of activities to be found in Montessori classrooms. It is intended to provide links for parents and practitioners who may not be so familiar with Montessori practice and to give a re-assurance that the Montessori approach offers children rich opportunities for exploration, learning and development.

Personal, Social and Emotional Development

Early learning goals as identified in the statutory guidance to the EYFS By the end of the EYFS children should:	Examples of Montessori practice Children:
Disposition and Attitudes • Continue to be interested, excited and motivated to learn.	• Are helped to settle into routines of the setting. • Undertake accessible activities. • Are encouraged to make choices. • Are given an explanation of 'how the room or classroom works'.

Early learning goals as identified in the statutory guidance to the EYFS By the end of the EYFS children should:	Examples of Montessori practice Children:
• Be confident to try new activities, initiate ideas and speak in a familiar group.	• Select activities spontaneously. • Are curious about new activities being undertaken by older peers, introduced by teachers and ready to try them. • Contribute to discussion with teachers and other children around the nature table, in the book or art corner, when sharing activities with the group.
• Maintain attention, concentrate, and sit quietly when appropriate.	• Concentrate when working on a self-chosen activity. • Are involved and take turns when working within a group. • Are able to listen to a story. • Begin meditation in yoga, during the 'Silence Game'. • Are able to listen to explanations.
Self-confidence and Self-esteem • Respond to significant experiences, showing a range of feelings when appropriate.	• Teachers ensure that children are given rich opportunities to respond to a range of experiences which reflect their feelings. The response celebrated and recorded where appropriate.
• Have a developing awareness of their own needs, views and feelings, and be sensitive to the needs, views and feelings of others.	• Are encouraged to take part in discussions and negotiations. • Are encouraged to show their needs, views and feelings when these present themselves.
• Have a developing respect for their own cultures and beliefs and those of other people.	• Discuss and develop a growing awareness of other cultures through projects.

Early learning goals as identified in the statutory guidance to the EYFS By the end of the EYFS children should:	*Examples of Montessori practice* Children:
Making Relationships • Form good relationships with adults and peers.	• Are able to settle well in the mornings. • Are able to share ideas, food, toys and materials with peers and adults in the setting. • Show politeness and consideration for friends, peers and adults. • Respond appropriately to key persons and other adults and peers in the setting.
• Work as part of a group or class, taking turns and sharing fairly, understanding that there needs to be agreed values and codes of behaviour for groups of people, including adults and children, to work together harmoniously.	• Are able to gradually accept the principles of sharing and caring for the classroom so that it can be used freely by everyone. • Show growing awareness of the needs of the group. • Respond to positive models of behaviour.
Behaviour and Self Control • Understand what is right, what is wrong and why.	• Are able to follow the expected code of behaviour and learn about why this is important.
• Consider the consequences of their words and actions for themselves and others.	• Learn about the consequences of their behaviour as events occur.
Self Care • Dress and undress independently and manage their personal hygiene.	• Have a growing ability to put on a coat to go outside or to go home, to use the toilet and wash their hands after using the toilet, before eating a snack or lunch, when returning into the classroom from outside. • Know about personal hygiene such as cleaning their teeth, brushing hair and so on.

Early learning goals as identified in the statutory guidance to the EYFS By the end of the EYFS children should:	Examples of Montessori practice Children:
Self Care (*cont.*) • Select and use activities and resources independently.	• Are able to use the favourable environment fully, engaging in all areas of the classroom, playing alone and with friends.
Sense of Community • Understand that people have different needs views, cultures and beliefs that need to be treated with respect.	• Take part in discussion during small group time, but also as incidents occur in the nursery. • Learn to put activities away to that they are ready for others. • Undertake project work on festivals, people and animals of the world.
• Understand that they can expect others to treat their needs, views, cultures and beliefs with respect.	• Have teachers who are role models • Show respect for each other's activities. • Show general respect and polite behaviour towards each other.

Communications, Language and Literacy

Early learning goals as identified in the statutory guidance to the EYFS By the end of the EYFS children should:	Examples of Montessori practice Children:
Language and Communication • Interact with others, negotiating plans and activities and taking turns in conversations.	• Are encouraged to express their ideas and contribute to conversations. • Participate in sharing of ideas and experiences in the book corner and art area and during role play.

Early learning goals as identified in the statutory guidance to the EYFS By the end of the EYFS children should:	Examples of Montessori practice Children:
Language and Communication (*cont.*)	• Choose to play group games such as animal loo. • Participate in block play, role-play and outdoor play.
• Enjoy listening to and using spoken and written language, and readily turn to it in their play and learning.	• Share books either on one to one basis or in a small group. • Listen to guidance on how to use materials, participate in cooking and other small group activities. • Have extensive one-to-one conversations with each other and adults.
• Sustain attentive listening, responding to what they have heard with relevant comments, questions and actions.	• Participate in story time, during group activities engage in attentive listening. • Listen to instructions given by adults and peers. • Participate in the 'Silence Game'. • Participate in 'I Spy', and 'Odd Man Out'. • Respond to science experiments and observations of the environment.
• Listen with enjoyment, and respond to stories, songs and other music, rhymes and poems and make up their own stories, songs, rhymes and poems.	• Participate and enjoy listening to stories. • Take advantage of the freedom of choice in the classroom which encourages enjoyments and creative use of language during book reading, role play and music time.

Early learning goals as identified in the statutory guidance to the EYFS By the end of the EYFS children should:	Examples of Montessori practice Children:
Language and Communication (*cont.*) • Extend their vocabulary, exploring the meanings and sounds of new words.	• Participate in three period lessons to extend their vocabulary. • Participate in small group activities, in story time, make books and use books on the project table. • Name objects in the environment, both inside and outside.
• Speak clearly and audibly with confidence and control and show awareness of the listener.	• Participate during small group time, converse at snack time and during the day. • Are polite role-models and have expectations of polite behaviour from each other. • Use language to negotiate 'what they would like or need'.
Language for Thinking • Use language to imagine and recreate roles and experiences.	• Play with the 'farm', 'hospital' or any other small world play available in the setting. • Engage in a spontaneous role-play both inside and outside. • Play with dinosaurs and other model animals. • Use language and comment on what they enjoy, observe, create.
• Use talk to organise, sequence and clarify thinking, ideas, feelings and events.	• Engage with block-play, practical life, sensorial and role-play areas. • Negotiate during spontaneously chosen activities.
Linking Sounds and Letters • Hear and say sounds in words in the order in which they occur.	• Participate in games such as 'I Spy' and 'Odd Man Out'. • Build words with a large movable alphabet.

Early learning goals as identified in the statutory guidance to the EYFS By the end of the EYFS children should:	*Examples of Montessori practice* Children:
Linking Sounds and Letters (*cont.*) • Link sounds to letters, naming and sounding the letters of the alphabet.	• Can recognise the letters of the alphabet and the sound they make using the sandpaper letters. • Recognise their own and other children's names by the initial. • Use the letter tray and letter made of sandpaper. • Play sound games.
• Use their phonic knowledge to write simple regular words and make phonetically plausible attempts at more complex words.	• Use word building to blend and segment with large movable alphabet. • Write titles on artwork and make books and write their own ideas in them.
Reading • Explore and experiment with sounds, words and text.	• Play rhyming and alliteration games. • Label objects, own work and make books.
• Retell narratives in the correct sequence, drawing on language patterns of stories.	• Use puppets and props to re-tell stories. • Follow up on a story started by someone else.
• Read a range of familiar and common words and simple sentences independently.	• Label objects and read the labels. • Read labels in the classroom and children's names. • Read word cards, lists, phrase and sentence strips.
• Know that print carries meaning and, in English, is read form left to right and top to bottom.	• Use and care for books appropriately. • Enjoy using books and share them with others.

Early learning goals as identified in the statutory guidance to the EYFS By the end of the EYFS children should:	Examples of Montessori practice Children:
Reading (*cont.*) • Show an understanding of the elements of stories, such as main character, sequence of events and openings, and how information can be found in non-fiction texts to answer questions about where, who, why and how.	• Are encouraged to make up stories with the help of objects. • Are encouraged to 'write' stories with the help of pictures or objects found in the setting.
Writing • Use their phonic knowledge to write simple regular words and make phonetically plausible attempts at more complex words.	• Use the writing area. • Are supported in emergent writing. • Write as part of role-play activities. • Record observations of nature.
• Attempt writing for different purposes, using features of different forms such a lists, stories and instructions.	• Use the writing area. • Are supported in emergent writing. • Write as part of role-play activities. • Record observations of nature.
• Write their own names and other things such as labels and captions, and begin to form simple sentences, sometimes using punctuation.	• Write their own name on painting and in workbooks. • Annotate their work.
Handwriting • Use a pencil and hold it effectively to form recognisable letters, most of which are correctly formed.	• Are introduced to insets for design. • Have access to paints and the art area. • Are encouraged to form letters by feeling sandpaper shapes.

Problem Solving, Reasoning and Numeracy

Early learning goals as identified in the statutory guidance to the EYFS By the end of the EYFS children should:	*Examples of Montessori practice* Children:
Numbers as Labels and for Counting • Say and use number names in order in familiar contexts.	• Join in rhymes, use counting books and count, for example: the number of children present, days of the week, number of spoons of ingredients when cooking.
• Count reliably up to ten everyday objects.	• Count number rods, pegs, spindles, counters, and other objects in the setting.
• Recognise numerals 1 to 9.	• Use sandpaper numerals and a spindle box, numbers cards, the birthday display and calendar.
• Use developing mathematical ideas and methods to solve practical problems.	• Play the 'snake game' to name number bonds of ten, play dominoes. • Make symmetrical, regular and irregular structures with blocks. • Are helped to find out what happens if objects are organised in pairs, sets, or taken away. • Use puzzles. • Explore sensorial materials.
Calculating • In practical activities and discussion, begin to use the vocabulary involved in adding and subtracting.	• Are introduced to the concept of addition and subtraction within everyday activities such an artwork or when building with blocks.

Early learning goals as identified in the statutory guidance to the EYFS By the end of the EYFS children should:	Examples of Montessori practice Children:
Calculating (cont.) • Use language such as 'more' or 'less' to compare two numbers.	• Count the number of spoons, raisins or biscuits taken at snack time or lunch-time. • Count in context of everyday activities such a group time or going outside.
• Find one more or one less than a number from one to ten.	• Use a number line, short bead stairs and the addition and subtraction strip board to count and explore numbers.
• Begin to relate addition to combining two groups of objects and subtraction to 'taking away'.	• Are introduced to the snake game and addition and subtraction with short bead stairs. • Use counting during role-play such as 'shop'.
Shape, Space and Measures • Use language such as 'greater', 'smaller', 'heavier', or 'lighter' to compare quantities.	• Use all the sensorial activities, especially the geometric solids, the geometric cabinet and the binomial and trinomial cube.
• Talk about, recognise and recreate simple patterns.	• Use constructive triangles, tessellations, blocks, beads, art area, songs and dancing, and fabrics, to recognise and create patterns.
• Use language such as 'circle' or 'bigger' to describe the shape and size of solids and flat shapes.	• Use all the sensorial activities, particularly those using geometric solids and the geometric cabinet.
• Use everyday words to describe position.	• Use outdoor activities to discuss position. • Use the preposition box. • Use the mapping game.

Knowledge and Understanding of the World

Early learning goals as identified in the statutory guidance to the EYFS By the end of the EYFS children should:	*Examples of Montessori practice* Children:
Exploration and Investigation • Investigate objects and materials by using all of their senses as appropriate.	• Participate in project work such as my body or transport. • Investigate the nature table displays, planting and gardening.
• Find out about, and identify, some features of living things, objects and events they observe.	• Participate in project work such as seasons, continents. • Have discussion in relation to activities available in the cultural areas of the classroom.
• Look closely at similarities, differences, patterns and change.	• Observe nature. • Find out about life cycles and the needs of plants, animals and people. • Learn about the consequences of their behaviours in relations to plants, animals, the environment.
• Ask questions about why things happen and how things work.	• Have opportunities to ask questions which relate to displays on the nature table and to individual and group work with activities presented within projects.
Designing and Making • Build and construct with a wide range of objects, selecting appropriate resources and adapting their work where necessary.	• Use block play and the Roman Arch. • Use craft activities. • Use carpentry tools and resources. • Participate in cooking.
• Select the tools and techniques they need to shape, assemble and join materials they are using.	• Have access to art area always set up with a wide range of resources, both for art and craft activities.

Early learning goals as identified in the statutory guidance to the EYFS By the end of the EYFS children should:	Examples of Montessori practice Children:
ICT • Find out about and identify the uses of everyday technology and use information and communication technology and programmable toys to support their learning.	• Have use of tape recorder and story and song tapes. • Have use of a typewriter, digital camera or telephone. • Are introduced to programmable toys such as Pixi. • Use technology such as mixers, beaters, hammers and screwdrivers for cooking and repairs. • May have access to appropriate software on the nursery computer.
Time • Find out about past and present events in their own lives, and in those of their families and other people they know.	• Discuss what is important to them. • Discuss the daily routine as presented with the calendar. • Discuss life cycles and make timelines. • Explore photographs.
Place • Observe, find out about and identify features in the place they live and the natural world.	• Observe and explore the garden. • Talk about their town, village and where things are. • Talk about the places they use and visit such as the supermarket, the library, the museum, train or bus station.
• Find out about their environment, and talk about those features they like and dislike.	• Discuss the walks such as to the library or playground. • Make up mapping games relevant to the local environment.
Communities • Begin to know about their own cultures and beliefs and those of other people.	• Celebrate birthdays and festivals. • Experience inclusive learning environment where everyone is respected.

Physical Development

Early learning goals as identified in the statutory guidance to the EYFS By the end of the EYFS children should:	Examples of Montessori practice Children:
Movement and Space • Move with confidence, imagination and in safety.	• Participate in music and movement. • Use outdoor equipment in the garden or regularly visit the local playground.
• Move with control and coordination.	• Do yoga or play games such as 'Who is Afraid of Mr Wolf'. • Participate in 'Walking on the Line' games. • Participate in group activities. • Use bicycles, tunnels and obstacle courses. • Use snack and art areas.
• Travel round, under, over and through balancing and climbing equipment.	• Use bicycles, climbing frames, slides and tunnels for riding, climbing and crawling. • Dance. • Play 'Walking on the Line' games. • Use climbing apparatus and balancing beams.
• Show awareness of space, of themselves and of others.	• Use the classroom and outdoor space. • Move with respect for others.
Health and Bodily Awareness • Recognise the importance of keeping healthy, and those things which contribute to this.	• Are offered healthy snacks. • Talk about food during lunch-time. • Participate in project work about food and its benefits.
• Recognise the changes that happen in their bodies when they are active.	• Participate in project work about our bodies, how they work, what makes us healthy and who helps us to be healthy.

Early learning goals as identified in the statutory guidance to the EYFS By the end of the EYFS children should:	Examples of Montessori practice Children:
Using Equipment and Materials • Use a range of small and large equipment.	• Use practical life activities both inside and outside – such as gardening, carpentry, cooking, art activities.
• Handle tools, objects, construction and malleable materials safely and with increasing control.	• Use practical life materials. • Use art and craft area. • Use carpentry sets.

Creative Development

Early learning goals as identified in the statutory guidance to the EYFS By the end of the EYFS children should:	Examples of Montessori practice Children:
Being Creative – responding to experiences, expressing and communicating ideas • Respond in a variety of ways to what they see, hear, smell, touch and feel.	• Refine their senses through the sensorial activities in the setting. • Have opportunities to make stories, draw, paint, sing songs and dance.
• Express and communicate their ideas, thoughts and feelings by using a widening range of materials, suitable tools, imaginative and role-play, movement, designing and making, and a variety of songs and musical instruments.	• Are encouraged to express their thoughts and feelings through drawing, painting, using a range of crafts and by dancing. Singing, making up stories and poems. • Participate in spontaneous imaginative and role-play. • Are encouraged to think creatively.

Early learning goals as identified in the statutory guidance to the EYFS By the end of the EYFS children should:	*Examples of Montessori practice* Children:
Explore Media and Materials • Explore colour, texture, shape, form and space in two or three dimensions.	• Explore sensorial activities. • Participate in a range of art and craft activities. • Play with blocks. • Engage in spontaneous and planned activities.
Creating Music and Dance • Recognise and explore how sounds can be changed, sing simple songs from memory, recognise repeated sounds and sound patterns, and match movements to music.	• Participate in spontaneous and organised singing. • Participate in music and movement activities. • Play music games. • Have access to musical instruments.
Developing Imagination and Imaginative Play • Use their imaginations in art and design, stories, music, dance, imaginative and role-play.	• Have opportunities to free expression in art and craft activities. • Dance to music. • Use prepared and spontaneously chosen props. • Participate in organised and spontaneous role-play. • Make up stories during practical life activities when block building, playing with the farm, dolls house or hospital, and during dressing up and when outside.

Appendix 2

Montessori activities and materials

These materials provide learning opportunities for children between the ages of two to six years. They can be purchased from Absorbent Minds – this supplier offers a comprehensive range of Montessori equipment from babies to twelve years of age. Their products range in quality and also in price, and those interested in purchasing Montessori materials have the opportunity to select the less expensive version, which may be appropriate for home use. On the other hand, a Montessori nursery school may choose the more expensive product because it will be used extensively by the children in their setting. The company website is fully illustrated and items for sale are organised according to areas of learning. Therefore, readers should be able to find pictures for most of the activities and materials listed below.

Practical life

Coordination of movement

- pouring, with jugs, small containers, strainers, funnels;
- transferring, with spoons, scoops, tongs, pipettes, droppers;
- estimating, sorting and matching.

These activities develop wrist flexibility, fine motor skills, hand–eye coordination, dexterity.

Opening and closing

- opening a variety of containers, including those in the activity areas in the classroom

- opening boxes, bottle lids; undoing padlocks, nuts, bolts.

These activities develop wrist flexibility (useful in writing).

Classroom skills

- cutting, using a variety of narrow paper strips;

- threading, using a range of beads from large to small;

- sewing, using sewing cards initially and progressing to use of a needle and thread;

- plaiting, using different colours of cord to highlight the pattern of the plait;

- folding, to make an envelope or book, to wrap a parcel, to fold cloths and clothes used in the classroom;

- using glue, paper clips, stapler, hole punch, date stamp.

These activities develop fine motor movement, particularly a pincer grip (useful in writing and art).

Personal independence and hygiene

- washing hands

- using the toilet

- cleaning teeth

- using the nail brush

- putting on a coat

- putting on shoes or Wellingtons

- using a dressing frame to do up and undo buttons, laces, bows, buckles, zips.

These activities help develop skills of everyday classroom participation.

Contributing towards upkeep of the classroom

- washing, scrubbing tables and chairs, washing dusters, washing dishes (after a snack or lunch);

- polishing – glass, brass, silver, wood, mirror, shoes;

- sweeping, dusting, wiping tables;

- setting the table for lunch or snack;

- gardening and looking after plants and pets.

These activities develop dexterity and contribute towards social aware-ness and a sense of well-being (as the child helps to look after the classroom).

The senses

The materials listed below can:

- refine sensorial impressions gathered during the early days of life and help organise and classify them;

- be used for matching, pairing, sorting, sequencing (laying foundations for later work in mathematics);

- help develop understanding of one-to-one correspondence, seriation and patterns and prepare for study of geometry and algebra (by understanding shape and form);

- develop dexterity and hand–eye coordination;

- help develop understanding of two- and three-dimensional shapes (by feeling them) and appreciation of shapes and forms found in our environment.

Understanding of shape, size and their relationships

- knobbed cylinders

- pink tower

- broad stair

- long rods

- coloured cylinders.

Chromatic sense

Colour boxes:

- colour box 1 includes pairs of the primary colours

- colour box 2 includes eleven pairs of colours

- colour box 3 includes nine colours.

Understanding of geometry and algebra

- geometric solids and their bases, stereognostic bags;

- the presentation tray, geometric cabinet and cards, constructive triangles, tessellations

- binomial and trinomial cube.

Activities to refine tactile sense

- touch boards
- touch tablets
- touch fabrics.

Activities to refine understanding of weight

- baric tablets.

Activities to refine understanding of temperature

- thermic tablets
- thermic bottles.

Activities to refine auditory sense

- sound boxes
- Montessori bells.

Activities to refine the sense of smell

- smell bottles.

Activities to refine the sense of taste

* taste jars.

Mathematics

Children work with numbers, exploring both quantities and symbols, before being introduced to the decimal system and addition, subtraction, multiplication and division.

Counting 0 to 10

The child builds up an understanding of 0 to 10 by manipulating objects and associating these objects with the written symbol. The child begins to learn one-to-one correspondence and the sequential nature of numbers.

* large number rods

* sandpaper numerals

* number rods and cards

* spindle box

* cards and counters.

The decimal system

Golden beads (which can be replaced by the wooden decimal materials commercially produced) are used to introduce the hierarchies of the decimal system. Beads as well as numeral cards (which use colour to represent the given hierarchies and place value) are used.

Group operations with golden beads

These activities introduce addition, subtractions, multiplication and division through group games.

They reinforce knowledge of numbers to 10 and relationships of decimal hierarchies. They introduce the concept of changing from one decimal hierarchy to another.

They provide a tangible example of the principles behind the four operations, for example, that addition is a process in which we 'add several smaller quantities to make another, larger quantity'.

Counting 10 to 99

- Teen Boards (Seguin Board A) numbers 11–19 using new materials

- Ten Boards (Seguin Board B) numbers 10–99 using new materials

- bead chains 100/1000 conservation/reversibility of number.

Addition and subtraction of small numbers (1 to 19)

Addition activities

- snake game (number bonds to 10)

- number rods (addition equations)

- addition with short bead stair (recording answers)

- addition strip board – introducing adding on, practising recording.

Subtraction activities

- subtraction with short bead stair (subtraction equations)

- small number rods (recording answers).

Tables

Children start working on tables, still using objects that they manipulate.

Charts

These charts reinforce previous learning of the number operations and help children memorise answers to the equation.

- addition chart A and B
- subtraction chart A and B
- multiplication chart A and B
- division chart A and B.

Fractions

Children start to use the fraction materials, using the fraction symbols and combining them with the fraction pieces. They learn about numerators, denominators, equivalents and reduction.

Measurement

Children learn about measurement by using spoons, cups as well as scales to measure ingredients during cooking activities.

They also use the long rods as a unit of measurement and usually have access to a measuring tape.

Clocks and time recognition are usually introduced around the age of five.

Money is introduced during role play.

Literacy materials

Most of the literacy materials used are teacher-made.

Writing

Insets of design encourage pencil control, lightness of touch and contribute to letter formation.

Sandpaper letters introduce the child to letter sounds and shapes in a multi-sensory manner.

Large moveable alphabets make links between the letter shape and formation of words at the time when children may not have the motor ability to write words. Objects and pictures are used to help children identify suitable words for word building.

Reading

Most Montessori nursery schools organise their reading activities into colour-coded levels, starting with words that consist of a consonant followed by a vowel followed by a consonant such as mat, pin, box. These words are suited to further activities with 'onset and rime' and prepare children well to decode more complex words using blends, diagrams and phonograms.

Pink level reading

The first level of reading focuses on three letter words consisting of the regular pattern consonant, vowel, consonant (such as pin, cot, bib).

Blue level reading

When children are competent in decoding three letters words, they are introduced to initial and final blends, the schwa vowel, double consonants (such as st, fr-, fl-, pr-, -ck, -sh, sh-, -ch, ch-, -th, th-).

Resources for children following the same sequence of activities in both levels:

- Boxes 1 and 2 – word building with large moveable alphabet letters
- Box 3 – decoding words on word cards using objects
- Box 4 – supporting word cards with pictures
- Box 5 – decoding without props (a mystery box)
- word lists
- phrases
- sentences
- books.

Grammar

Grammar is introduced early in Montessori classrooms in support of the pink and blue level reading and with the help of colour-coding, which represents parts of speech.

Parts of speech are introduced through games, starting with nouns as labels that can be placed with objects in the classroom such as map, bin, rod.

- noun labels
- singular and plural boxes, introducing the formation of plurals by adding -s
- adjective labels
- noun and adjective games, highlighting the function of adjectives and their position
- verb games, acting out verbs
- preposition boxes, highlighting the function of prepositions

- farm boxes, building sentences based around the theme of a farm.

Green level reading

This level of reading requires competence at both the pink and blue levels. It focuses on one specific phonogram or diagraph such as -ar. The children work through the activities listed below before moving on to the next green box, which identifies new spellings.

- reading – supported by the use of pictures

- word building – spelling difficulty is highlighted by the colour of letters, which represent the given phonogram or diagraph

- word lists

- phrases

- sentences

- books.

Cultural studies

Most of the cultural materials used in the Montessori classroom are teacher-made.

The globes and puzzle maps used in geography can be obtained from Montessori suppliers. These materials contribute to the child's greater understanding of the natural and created world and encourage observation, exploration and investigation.

Biology

- a nature table, reflecting the seasons and children's interests

- models such as farm, wild and sea animals and birds

- pictures or plants, animals, habitats in their classifications

- terminology puzzles and cards identifying part of an animal or a plant
- life cycles.

Geography

- land, air and water boxes
- globes, showing land and water and the continents
- land forms and cards
- puzzle maps of the world and individual continents
- animals of the world
- flags
- artefact boxes and collections of pictures of children and their families from around the world
- mapping games.

History

Children are introduced to the concept of time.

- egg timers
- time lines
- calendars.

Science

Experiments that focus on investigating the properties of:

- the four elements (light, water, air, fire – fire is used with adult supervision only)

- magnetism
- electricity.

Bibliography

Bowlby, J. (1988) *Secure Base.* London: Penguin.

Britton, L. (1998) *Montessori: Play and Learn.* New York: Vermillion Press.

Bruce, T. (1991) *Time to Play in Early Childhood Education.* London: Hodder & Stoughton.

Bruce, T. (2005) *Early Childhood Education,* 3rd edn. London: Hodder Arnold.

Bruner, J. (1960) *The Process of Education.* Cambridge, MA: Harvard University Press.

Chattin-McNichols, J. (1992) *The Montessori Controversy.* New York: Delmar Publishers.

DCSF, Department for Children, School and Families (2008) *The Early Years Foundation Stage.* Annesley, UK: DCSF Publications.

DCSF, Department for Children, School and Families (2002) *Every Child Matters.* UK: The Stationery Office. Available at www.everychildmatters. gov.uk/uncrc

Duffy, M. and D. Duffy (2002) *Children of the Universe: Cosmic Education in the Montessori Elementary Classroom.* Hollidaysburgh, PA: Parent Child Press.

Gettman, D. (1987) *Basic Montessori: Learning Activities for Under-Fives.* Oxford: ABC-Clio.*

Gura, P., ed. (1992) *Exploring Learning: Young Children and Blockplay.* London: Paul Chapman.

Hainstock, E. (1978) *Essential Montessori*. New York: Plume Books.

Holt, J. (1967) *How Children Learn*. London: Penguin.

Jenkinson, S. (2002) *The Genius of Play*. Stroud: Hawthorn Press.

Kelly, A. V. (1989) *The Curriculum: Theory and Practice*. London: Paul Chapman Publishing.

Kramer, R. (1976) *Maria Montessori*. London: Montessori International Publishing.

Lawrence, L. (1998) *Montessori: Read and Write*. London: Ebury Press.

Liebeck, P. (1984) *How Children Learn Mathematics*. London: Penguin.

Lillard, P. P. (1972) *Montessori: A Modern Approach*. New York: Schocken Books.

Lillard, P. P. (1980) *Montessori in the Classroom*. New York: Schocken Books.

Lillard, P. P. (1996) *Montessori Today*. New York: Schocken Books.

Lillard, P. P. and Lillard Jessen, L. (2003) *Montessori from the Start*. New York: Schocken Books.

Loeffler, M. H., ed. (1992) *Montessori in Contemporary American Culture*. Portsmouth, NH: Heinemann.

Macleod-Brudenell, I., ed. (2004) *Advanced Early Years Care and Education*. Oxford: Heinemann.

MCI, Montessori Centre International (2006) *Montessori Philosophy, Module 1*. London: MCI.

Montanaro, S. Q. (1991) *Understanding the Human Being*. Mountain View, CA: Nienhuis Montessori USA.

Montessori, M. (1964) [1912] *The Montessori Method*. New York: Schocken Books.

Montessori, M. (1965) [1914] *Dr Montessori's Own Handbook*. New York: Schocken Books.

Montessori, M. (1966) [1936] *The Secret of Childhood*. Notre Dame, IN: Fides Publishers Ltd.

Montessori, M. (1988a) [1949] *The Absorbent Mind*. Oxford: ABC-Clio, Volume 1.*

Montessori, M. (1988b) [1912] *The Discovery of the Child* (originally published as *The Montessori Method*). Oxford: ABC-Clio, Volume 2.*

Montessori, M. (1989a) [1955] *The Formation of Man*. Oxford: ABC-Clio, Volume 3.*

Montessori, M. (1989b) [1961] *What You Should Know About Your Child*. Oxford: ABC-Clio, Volume 4.*

Montessori, M. (1989c) [1946] *Education for New World*. Oxford: ABC-Clio, Volume 5.*

Montessori, M. (1989d) [1948] *To Educate the Human Potential*. Oxford: ABC-Clio, Volume 6.*

Montessori, M. (1989e) [1979] *The Child, Society and the World*. Oxford: ABC-Clio, Volume 7.*

Montessori, M. (1989f) [1975] *The Child in the Family*. Oxford: ABC-Clio, Volume 8.*

Montessori, M. (1991) [1918] *The Advanced Montessori Method – Volume 1*. Oxford: ABC-Clio, Volume 9.*

Montessori, M. (1992) [1949] *Education and Peace*. Oxford: ABC-Clio, Volume 10.*

Montessori, M. (1994) [1948] *From Childhood and Adolescence*. Oxford: ABC-Clio, Volume 12.*

Montessori, M. (1995) [1916] *The Advanced Montessori Method – Volume 2*. Oxford: ABC-Clio, Volume 13.*

Montessori, M. (1997a) [1976] *Basic Ideas of Montessori's Educational Theory*. Oxford: ABC-Clio, Volume 14.*

Montessori, M. (1997b) *California Lectures of Maria, 1915*. Oxford: ABC-Clio, Volume 15.*

Montessori, M. Jnr (1992) [1976] *Education for Human Development*. Oxford: ABC-Clio, Volume 11*.

Montessori St Nicholas Charity (2008) The Guide to Early Years Foundation Stage in Montessori Settings. London: MSN.

Moyles, J., ed. (2005) The Excellence of Play. Buckingham/Philadelphia, PA: Open University Press.

MSA (2009) National Census, London: Montessori St. Nicholas Charity.

Piaget, J. (1962) Play, Dreams and Imitation in Childhood. London: Routledge & Kegan Paul.

Rich, D. et al. (2005) First Hand Experience: What Matters to Children: An Alphabet of Learning from the Real World. London: Rich Learning Opportunities.

Standing E. M. (1984) Maria Montessori: Her Life and Work. New York: Plume.

Stoll-Lillard, A. (2004) The Science Behind the Genius. New York: Oxford University Press.

Vygostsky, L. (1978) Mind in Society. Cambridge, MA: Harvard University Press.

Wolf, A. D. (1996) Nurturing the Spirit in Non-Sectarian Classrooms. Hollidaysburg, PA: Parent Child Press.

Please note that all the titles identified with * are now available from Montessori Pierson Publishing, Amsterdam.

eBooks – at www.eBookstore.tandf.co.uk

A library at your fingertips!

eBooks are electronic versions of printed books. You can store them on your PC/laptop or browse them online.

They have advantages for anyone needing rapid access to a wide variety of published, copyright information.

eBooks can help your research by enabling you to bookmark chapters, annotate text and use instant searches to find specific words or phrases. Several eBook files would fit on even a small laptop or PDA.

NEW: Save money by eSubscribing: cheap, online access to any eBook for as long as you need it.

Annual subscription packages

We now offer special low-cost bulk subscriptions to packages of eBooks in certain subject areas. These are available to libraries or to individuals.

For more information please contact webmaster.ebooks@tandf.co.uk

We're continually developing the eBook concept, so keep up to date by visiting the website.

www.eBookstore.tandf.co.uk